I0815792

ma

The Japanese Secret to Contemplation and Calm

edited by KEN RODGERS
and JOHN EINARSEN

TUTTLE Publishing

Tokyo | Rutland, Vermont | Singapore

This book is dedicated to the memory of Ken Rodgers (1952–2024), poet, farmer, impresario, pilgrim, doting grandfather, and managing editor of Kyoto Journal *for nearly forty years.*

Contents

Introduction

what is ma?

by Alex Kerr

Sometime in the early 1980s, after art collector David Kidd had moved to his house at Kujoyama overlooking Kyoto, David and I came up with the idea for a play. Every time I visited Kujoyama, we'd add a bit more to the storyline. It was to be called *The Master of Ma*.

It began as a spoof on Kyoto's hereditary houses of tea ceremony, Noh drama and so forth, cocooned in their layers of mystery and secrets. Imbued with Chinese cynicism, David was amused by the worshipful seriousness with which the teachings of these schools were viewed by devotees. According to David, there had been an original Master of Ma, who had brought ma over from China to Kyoto in the fourteenth century. Ma was kept in a box, and that box was enshrined in the headquarters of the Master of Ma, whose school was hugely successful and now taught ma to millions of loyal followers across the nation.

In our play, it was never made clear what was taught or what was learned, and certainly not what ma was. Nobody except the Master of Ma, now in his thirty-seventh generation, ever knew what was inside the box.

As we expanded on the idea over the years, adding hilarious comments from David, we began to realize that this was a deeper story than the joke we had originally envisioned. After David's death in 1997, I went on developing it, eventually turning the play into a novel. It's still being written. As the story has unfolded, we're getting some intriguing hints, but it's now over forty years and counting, and we still don't know what's in the box.

Whether the ma of *The Master of Ma* turns out to be the same as the ma presented in this book is not clear. It might be, but then again it might not. What we can say, is that ma is perhaps the single most elusive Japanese aesthetic idea that ever was.

As readers of the following essays will see, ma can mean "the space between things," "the time between things," the "placement of things," and at the same time "the emptiness where there are no things." It's a way of structuring time and space that's asymmetrical, apparently chaotic, and yet it has its inner rules. Ma in one form or another is a core element of every traditional Japanese art, from Noh drama and koto to architecture and gardens. Ma is the emptiness of sand and moss; it's the scattered stones in the emptiness. Ma is a phrase of music; it's the pause between phrases.

The emptiness, and the unexpected but inexplicably pleasing placement of things within the emptiness—it's fair to say that this is the single most powerful element behind the appeal of Japanese art. It has fascinated the world since Japan opened up to the outside world in the nineteenth century, and does so even more strongly today. The spatial and temporal sense of ma makes Japanese art calm and meditative. At the same time, the unforeseen and quirky play of space and time is endlessly entertaining.

While ma has been much written about, both by Japanese and foreigners, this collection is perhaps the most definitive book yet published on the subject. The contributing writers and artists cover a wide range, with special emphasis on gardens, but also including photography, sculpture, painting, calligraphy, martial arts, tea ceremony, music and poetry, and reaching beyond into Buddhist philosophy. Pico Iyer has even written about ma in conversation.

How little needs to be spoken. I've found that as I grow older, I'm becoming fond of the silences when I'm in Japan. People from other countries have so much to say, so much to ask. In Japan, the rhythm of comment and response—the ma—takes over, and empty silences can just be.

Actually, David Kidd, who was very persuasive, once got the Master of Ma to lend him the box for a weekend, and I got a look inside. Not inside the inner box, tied with knots that only the Master can ever unravel. But I did manage a peek into the outer box. What I learned is that Ma exists in three types: Primal Ma, Artistic Ma and Cultural Ma.

Primal Ma is something that happens instinctively in Japan. I find it the windows of *kura* storehouses, where a large window in a kura wall is joined by one or two smaller ones inserted here and there at incongruous spots. It probably happened for random reasons. First they built one window, and later they felt like adding another. Critically, it never entered anyone's head that they should be lined up just so. They put that second window where they wanted it, not caring whether the second window was aligned with the first, or had any discernible relationship to it at all. In China or the West you couldn't usually get away with that. Japan is very forgiving, even encouraging, of randomness.

There's a tendency when people talk about ma, to assume that it's all planned, there are deep reasons for why things are placed the way they are. It doesn't seem right to accept that these placements came about by sheer happenstance. And yet, chaos, and taking joy in chaos, lies at the root of Primal Ma. It's the randomness of those windows that pleases the soul, in a way that a perfect symmetrical row never would.

Artistic Ma is when it's done on purpose. Over and over again in Japanese culture, we find that when space or objects become organized, balanced or logical, people want to break it up, experiment by inserting some artificial chaos. The artist or architect polishes his intuition for randomness and acquires the skill of how to choose what is "right."

As a calligraphy collector, I have been intrigued by the art of *chirashi* ("scattering"). Calligraphers using the soft flowing lines of the *kana* alphabet will scatter words or phrases up and down across the page. After the sixteenth century (especially in the writing of women), the scattering got so complex that in order to decipher these calligraphies, we have to number the scattered bits word by word and phrase by phrase. Phrase number 3 is up high to the right; number 4 is low to the left; number 5 might follow number 21. It's chaotic, but the scattered lines of script are intriguing, alluring. The art of chirashi supersedes the art of calligraphy.

Another form of chirashi is found in *shikishi* screens. Court nobles in Kyoto used to hold poetry contests, during which they inscribed poems on small slips of square or rectangular paper. The squarish ones were called *shikishi*, the rectangular *tanzaku*, and these were highly valued for their elegant calligraphy. However, collectors of these, as well as of decorated old fans, had the "stamp collector's problem," namely, how to display a lot of little things. You could preserve them in albums, where they would lie in darkness only to be seen by the occasional connoisseur, and what's the fun of that? The solution was to mount them dramatically on gold screens by pasting the shikishi and tanzaku erratically over the surface. Nothing exactly lines up with anything else, but somehow it succeeds, the scattering itself again becoming a work of art. The nearly-but-not-quite-matching lines of square shikishi and rectangular tanzaku form satisfying Mondrianesque patterns. Or 90-degree angles might be abandoned altogether, as when fans pasted on a screen are shown flipping and flying through the air or drifting down a painted stream. That's the fun of it.

"Fun" is the missing word in the essays of this book, although that might be because our writers, reveling in ma, have taken the fun for granted. Artistic Ma happens when someone thinks, "Let's break things up with the unexpected! Twist the space, add a gap where we didn't see one coming." In the late sixteenth century, tea masters sought liberation from the pillar-and-post system of traditional architecture, where space is measured out tatami by modular tatami. They invented irregular tatami, called *daime*. A daime might be one half, or three quarters of a normal tatami mat, and in order to fit something like that in, the whole building had to be altered. Tearooms became more challenging, more interesting.

The stepping stones along the "dewy path" of a tea garden must never be too regular. Larger or smaller, set a bit farther to the left or right, they literally keep you on your toes. David Kidd used to say, "They shouldn't be called strolling gardens, they should be called tottering gardens!" Or course, stone placement goes far beyond dewy paths and is core to Japanese gardens in general. The earliest book on gardens, *Sakuteiki*, published in the eleventh century, calls garden designing *ishi wo tateru koto*, "the act of standing up stones."

"Standing up stones" might be better translated as "burying stones." Stones in Japanese gardens tend to be low-lying, hugging the earth, rather than soaring upward as in Chinese gardens. That gives them the quality of "just happening to be there," which is one reason why Japanese gardens are so restful. And yet, they didn't just happen to be there. An artist dove deep into the dark pool of his intuition, and then manipulated the space by setting a slightly lower rounder stone here, and a higher pointier one over there, with plenty of emptiness to swim around in. He did chirashi with stones.

Flower master Kawase Toshiro once told me that the art of flowers was a matter of "artifice, artifice, artifice—until it finally looks natural." That's Artistic Ma.

Then we have Cultural Ma. This is what happens to Artistic Ma if you go on doing it long enough. Over centuries, the gaps and odd rhythms become established and ritualized, as in Noh drama and tea ceremony. It's not for Noh dancers or tea practitioners to capriciously create brand new ma. It's all been codified long ago.

This sounds like the opposite of the free-spirited randomness from which it all began. But in fact, Cultural Ma may be the deepest ma of them all. It can take decades to master the subtleties, because while there are plenty of rules—a lifetime's study of rules—and most of them aren't written down anywhere. Even when they have been, it doesn't do you much good. You just have to practice the art form long enough to get the feel. At one point I studied *kotsuzumi* (the Noh shoulder drum), and while I loved the sound of the two notes when striking the drum, *pon* and *ta*, I couldn't get the hang of the ma. My pon and ta were never right. I got to where I could follow the basic rhythm, but the tiny, almost infinitesimal variations between notes baffled me completely. And without these, you aren't playing Noh music. In the end I gave up the kotsuzumi.

It turns out that mastery of the codified forms in all their refinement is not enough. As with Western classical music, the basics may be prescribed, but the practitioner must then create his own space and time. The tighter the restrictions, the more delicately can an artist stretch the ma a little this way or that to create something original. There's always room to insert an instant of quiet and emptiness, or to add a touch of pleasing chaos.

In John McGee and Alexandre Avdulov's essay on tea, ma is described as a flow from start to finish, taking guests literally out of this world and onto a higher plane. Famously, the expression *ichigo ichie* ("one time, one meeting") is used to describe tea, referring to the combination of guests, season, utensils and garden, all unique to that moment. The relationship of these things to each other adds up to ma—random yet meditative and restful, familiar yet surprising—even when you know in advance what to expect.

As to *The Master of Ma*, I'm working now on how to unravel the cords that bind the inner box. This may take a while, as only the Master has ever been granted this knowledge. Meanwhile, I've got tea gatherings and photography exhibitions to attend, Noh drama performances to watch, and Zen gardens to visit. Maybe somewhere among these I'll find the secret.

ma—place, space, void

by Gunter Nitschke

Length of time depends upon our ideas.
Size of space hangs upon our sentiments.
For one whose mind is free from care,
A day will outlast the millennium.
For one whose heart is large,
A tiny room is as the space between heaven and earth.[1]

Place is the product of lived space and lived time, a reflection of our states of mind and heart. In the original Chinese, the above poem ends with the character 間, which in Japanese is pronounced chiefly as *ma*.

Originally, this character consisted of the pictorial sign for "moon" (月)—not the present-day "sun" (日)—under the sign for "gate" (門). For a Chinese or Japanese person using language consciously, this ideogram, depicting a delicate moment of moonlight

1. Translated from *Saikontan* (Vegetable Roots Talks), Yuhodo, Tokyo, 1926

streaming through a chink in the entranceway, fully expresses the two simultaneous components of a sense of place: the objective, given aspect; and the subjective, felt aspect.

The translation of ma as "place" is my own.[2] The dictionaries say "space," but historically the notion of place precedes our contemporary idea of space as a measurable area. Architectural theorists accept this: "In [our] understanding of nature we . . . recognize the origin of the concept of space as a system of places."[3] My translation was selected in part to get away from the rendering of ma as "imaginary space" by Itoh Teiji[4]; this deals only with the subjective aspect, without doing justice to the full spectrum of use and meaning which this venerable character represents.

It must be stressed that a "sense of place" does not negate an objective awareness of the static or homogenous quality of topological space. Rather, it infuses the objective space with an additional subjective awareness of lived, existential, non-homogenous space. It also incorporates a recognition of the activities which "take place" in a particular space, and different meanings a place might have for various individuals or cultures. "Physical appearance, activities, and meanings are the raw material of the identity of places . . ."[5]

From the hundreds of uses of the character ma in traditional and modern Japanese, I have selected a few which I present here in order of increasing complexity of meaning.

---

2. Nitschke, G. "Ma—The Japanese Sense of Place," *Architectural Design*, London, March 1966
3. Norberg-Schulz, *Christian. Genius Loci—Towards a Phenomenology of Architecture*, Rizzoli, New York, 1980.
4. Itoh Teiji, *Nihon dizain ron* (Discourses on Japanese Design), Kashima Kenkyujo, Tokyo, 1966. "*Nihon no toshi kukan*" (Japanese Urban Space), Kenchiku Bunka 12, Tokyo, 1963
5. Ralph, Edward, *Place and Placelessness*, Pion Ltd, London, 1976.

THE DOMAIN OF OBJECTIVITY

ma: the one-dimensional realm

hari-ma
beam span

Here ma denotes a line in space, a measure of length or distance. From ancient times, Japanese architecture was based on wooden post-and-beam construction. The distance between the centerlines of successive posts—the *hashira-ma* (橋ラマ)—evolved into the basic structural unit of the traditional Japanese wooden house. To signify this carpentry measure, the character is pronounced *ken*. (Over time, and in different regions of the country, the ken varied in length from about ten to six feet [three to two meters]). By the sixteenth century, all column sizes and timber dimensions were expressed as fractions or multiples of ken. The sizes of the rush mats which evolved into tatami were also originally derived from the ken.

東京と京都の間 (*Tokyo to Kyoto no aida*)
Between Tokyo and Kyoto

Standing alone and pronounced as *aida*, 間 denotes not only a straight-line distance between two points in space, but also a simultaneous awareness of both poles as individual units. Thus even in a simple one-dimensional use, the character ma exhibits its peculiar ambivalence, signifying both "distance" or "interstice" and "relatedness" or "polarity."[6]

---

6. LaFleur, William R. "Notes on Watsujii Tetsuro's Social Philosophy and the Arts: Ma in Man, Time and Space," unpublished paper, Topical Seminar on Time and Space in Japanese Culture, Cornell University, 1976.

ma: the two-dimensional realm

Ma combined with a number of tatami mats denotes area. For a Japanese, however, a reference to a room of a certain number of floor mats would also instantly call to mind a particular usage, interior makeup, decoration and height.[7]

Since the adoption of the tatami in Japanese residential architecture about five hundred years ago, there have been two ways of expressing land area: the *tsubo* (坪), an area one ken square measured from the centerlines of the columns; and *jo* (帖), the area covered by one tatami. Neither is an exact measure. The tsubo does not respect the thickness of the walls, while tatami sizes vary from region to region. For modern construction, the square meter is always used.

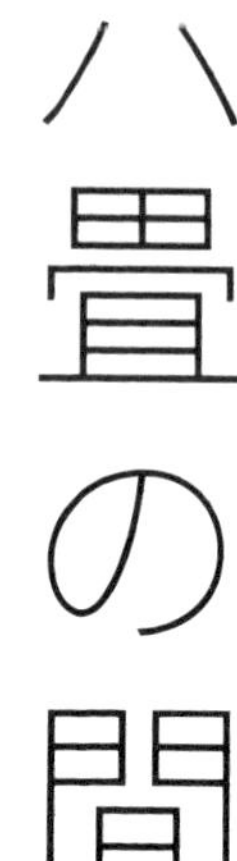

roku jo no ma
six-tatami room
(literally: six tatami area)

ma: the three-dimensional realm

The first character in this word originally stood for a "hole in the ground," and later took on its present meaning of a "hole in the universe" or "the sky." Ono Susumu[8] suggests that the ancient Japanese divided space vertically into two parts. One was *sora* (空, sky), which was understood as absence of content, emptiness. The other was *ame* or *ama* (天, heaven), which was the

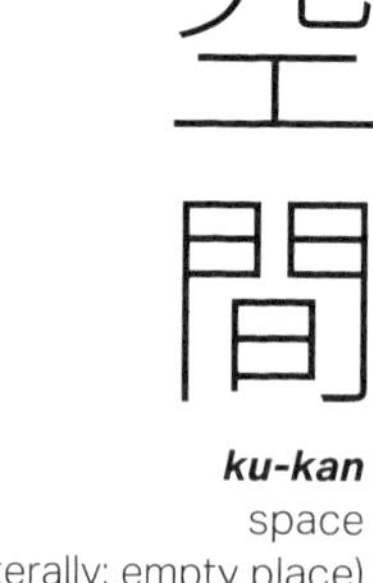

ku-kan
space
(literally: empty place)

7. For a detailed study of the relationship between a room size and its social use over history, see Kojiro Junichiro, "*Kokono-ma ron*" (The Nine-mat Room), in *SD: Space Design*, Tokyo, June 1969.
8. Ono Susumu, *Nihongo o sukanoboru* (Tracing the Origins of the Japanese Language), Chapter 2, Iwanami Shinsho, Tokyo, 1972.

opposite of *kuni* (国, region, realm, government) and thus meant an earthly area of habitation and rule.

Today the word *ku* is used for "empty" in the simple physical sense, and for "void" in Buddhist metaphysics. The compound *ku-kan* is of recent origin. It was coined to express the concept of three-dimensional objective space which was imported from the West, for which the Japanese language had no word of its own. (The Western concept was, and still is, inherently static and unchanging, without any dynamic sense of variation or human subjectivity. It is merely three-dimensional.)

Thus ku-kan compounds two characters which are charged with independent meanings by long Chinese and Japanese cultural traditions including Buddhism. These traditional meanings soon influenced the compound, yielding a meaning different from the original intent, and causing some obvious confusion in postwar architectural writing.

The structure of Japanese dictates a linguistic description of space different from that of European languages, as illustrated in the following combinations of ma with other characters.

土間 (*do-ma*)
Work space (literally: earth place), especially in farmhouses with stamped-earth floors

間引く (*ma-biku*)
To thin out (literally: to draw or pull space), making room for plants to grow

貸間 (*kashi-ma*)
Room to let

茶の間 (*cha-no-ma*)
Tearoom; denotes space in the home where guests are entertained or the family gathers

床の間 (*toko-no-ma*)
Display alcove in the traditional Japanese sitting or guest room for a scroll, flower arrangement or objet d'art. The toko-no-ma is at once a spatial and an aesthetic concept, and furthermore has an important social connotation in Japanese life. Classically it constitutes the unifying focus between host and guest, through an act of creation on the part of the host and an act of appreciation on the part of the guest.

虎の間 (*tora-no-ma*)
The Tiger Room (literally, place of tigers) is the name of a room in the abbot's quarters at Nanzenji in Kyoto. The dominant decorative motif on the sliding doors becomes the qualifier of the entire space, a common custom in mansions, castles, temples and present-day hotel ballrooms. The naming of places, man-made or natural, is a universal means of giving meaning and identity to a lived or existential space.

鏡の間 (*kagami-no-ma*)
Dressing room (literally: mirror room) separated from the Noh stage by a curtain. This is the place reserved for the magical transformation of the actor, via the donning of the spiritually charged Noh mask, and the meditation or inner-reflection involved in facing the full-length mirror.

ma: the four-dimensional realm

This is abstract time, with no indication of length, beginning or end. The *ji* character, which incorporates the radical for "sun," is said to have denoted "forward movement of the sun" in ancient China. In Japanese the character is also pronounced *toki*, perhaps from the old Japanese verb *toku*, to melt or dissolve. Thus "time" is expressed in Japanese

ji-kan
time
(literally: time-place)

as "space in flow," making time a dimension of space. Indeed, time is essential to human experience of place.

Here are a few modern Japanese phrases in which ma (sometimes pronounced kan) denotes stretches of time.

瞬間 (*shun-kan*)
A moment (literally: a blink or twinkle of time)

間に合う (*ma-ni-au*)
To be in time for (literally: to meet the time)

間もなく (*ma mo naku*)
Soon (literally: in no time)

Most cultures measure and express time in terms of intervals in space (or at least they did so before digital clocks replaced sundials and watchdials). It is not surprising then, that the same Japanese character, pronounced variously as ma or aida or kan, can be used to denote either temporal or spatial extension. Some examples:

相間 (*ai-no-ma*)
Literally: reciprocating place
1. A room in between
2. Interval, leisure

間近い (*ma-jikai*)
Literally: a close space
1. Close at hand (spatially)
2. Drawing near (temporally)

間者 (*kan-ja*)
Spy (literally: ma person); one who works in between known spaces or known hours

間男 (*ma-otoko*)
Adulterer (literally: ma man) one who makes love in between usual places or usual times

The dual relation of ma to space and time is not just semantic. It reflects the fact that all experience of space is a time-structured process, and all experience of time is a space-structured process.

When we look at a traditional Japanese scroll picture or *emakimono*, time is concretely present as our eyes follow a sequence of spatial events interrupted by writing. Our hands actually unroll the scroll, that is, "move the space" as time passes. Nothing could be more detrimental to the intended narrative process of viewing than a full simultaneous display of the scroll as a whole. In traditional Japanese paintings of palaces and gardens shown in the *fukinuke-yatai* or "blown-away rooftop" technique, time becomes part of our spatial experience as our eyes have to move from scene to scene in various adjacent spaces.

In traditional tourist manuals of famous scenic routes, which were sold as small books and could be unfolded into continuous-strip pictures often more than twenty feet (six meters) in length, another technique was used to represent space as a time-structured process. The spatial sights would be drawn above and below the continuous central road, shown as they would unfold themselves concretely over time to the traveler. Thus we end up with a "plan" of the route quite different from modern orthographic maps. In a Tokaido manual of the mid-1800s, for instance, Mount Fuji is represented about fifty times in various settings along the route.

We can find a similar presentation and understanding of space as a time- and mood-structured process in the layout of traditional Japanese stroll gardens and, on a smaller scale, in the placement of *tobi-ishi*, ("skipping stones") used to make garden paths. By a sophisticated placing of the stones, our foot movements can be slowed down, sped up, halted or turned in various directions. And with our legs, our eyes are manipulated, and our visual input from spatial phenomena is structured over time.

THE DOMAIN OF SUBJECTIVITY

ma: the realm of experience

Here a time/space metaphor is used to express a very personal, subjective notion. The phrase is used in everyday situations as well as in the arts. It means that a place or situation is uncomfortable, because of either the atmosphere (environmental or social) or one's own mood, with the result that one becomes self-conscious or embarrassed. A contemporary rendering might be "the vibes are bad."

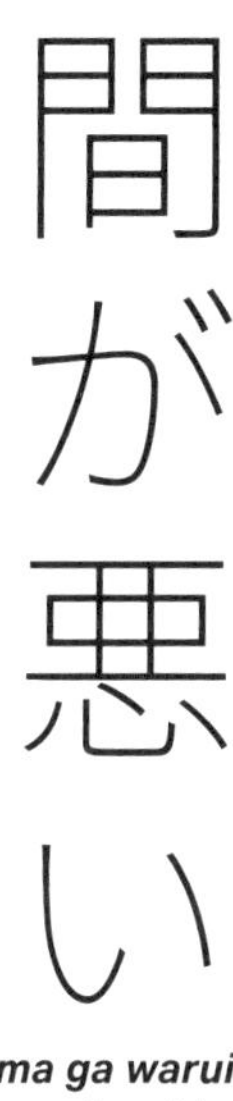

ma ga warui
I am uncomfortable, embarrassed
(literally: the placing is bad)

This shows us another side of the ma concept—the notion that animation is an essential feature of place. The animation may be something which is projected from one's subjective feelings; but it also may be some external, objective quality, the genius loci or spirit of the place, which projects itself into our minds. René Dubos has alluded to this duality: "I remember the mood of places better than their precise features because places evoke for me life situations rather than geographical sites."[9] The uses of ma point up the fact that the identity of a place is as much in the mind of the beholder as in its physical characteristics.

Many waka and haiku poems begin with a phrase that employs ma to paint the atmosphere of energy of the setting. Examples:

木の間 (*ko-no-ma*)
Among trees (literally: place/time/mood of trees)

9. Dubos, René. *A God Within*, Scribner's, New York, 1972.

波間 (*nami-ma*)
On waves (place/time/mood of waves)

岩間 (*iwa-ma*)
On rocks (place/time/mood of rocks)

ma: the realm of art

The previously mentioned *ma ga warui* or its opposite, *ma ga umai*, is often used as an aesthetic judgment of Japanese calligraphy or *sumi-e* painting. Compared with Western painting, these Sino-Japanese art forms involve large unpainted areas. Anyone practicing calligraphy soon realizes that proficiency lies not merely in mastering the form of the characters, but also in the relationship of the form to the surrounding non-form. This balance of form and space will always be taken into account in the final artistic judgment.

The proper appreciation of calligraphy also takes note of the dimension of time, for calligraphy is more than simple painting or drawing. It is an intricate mixture of poetry, dance and action painting. It is not only the placing of form into space, but also the marking of rhythm in time—the traces of the movement and speed of the brush.

In the area of the performing arts, the following is the typical phrase used to praise a performance of *rakugo*, the traditional comic storytelling genre:

話の間ごうまい (*hanashi no ma go umai*)
The timing (ma) of the story was excellent

The aesthetic quality of the rakugo performance depends as much or more on the time of the pauses as on the quality of the voice. The pause is both an interval in time and a bridge between sound and silence. The fifteenth-century poet Shinkei had this to say about ma in the recitation of poetry: “In linked verse, put your mind to what is not.”

Calligraphy in the grass style, meaning "mysterious and far away," painted by Kimura in 1983. (From *Sumi*, November 1983, Geijutsu Shimbunsha, Tokyo)

This admonition corresponds to the oft-quoted dictum on Noh acting by Zeami, the great formulator of the Noh plays: "What [the actor] does not do is of interest" (*Senu tokoro ga omoshiroki*). Indeed, Noh actor Komparu Kunio regards Noh as no more nor less than the art of ma: the staging is meant to "create a constantly transmuting, transforming space [ma] of action"; the acting, to do "just enough to create the ma that is a blank space-time where nothing is done": the music, to "exist in the negative, blank spaces generated by the actual sounds"; and the dance, to acquire "the technique of non-movement."[10]

Noh is the supreme expression of the art of ma, combining all the aspects that have so far been elaborated here into one great symphony. It epitomizes the traditional Japanese artistic preoccupation with dynamic balance between object and space, action and inaction, sound and silence, movement and rest.

間取り (*ma-dori*)
Design (literally: grasp of place)

The Japanese architect traditionally worked to "create a sense of place" (*ma-dori o tsukuru*). Implicit in this term, according to architect Seike Kyoshi[11], was the design not only of structural elements in space, but also of the variable arrangements for temporary uses which are so characteristic of the Japanese dwelling. By adding and removing sliding doors, windows, portable screens and other household utensils, the Japanese home is adapted to changing seasons, uses and social needs. Nowadays, unfortunately, the term *ma-dori*, so charged with connotations of place, has been replaced with an "exotic" imported term: *dizain* (design).

10. Komparu Kunio, *The Noh Theatre: Principles and Perspectives*, Weatherhill/Tankosha, Tokyo 1983.
11. Seike Kyoshi, "*Sumai to ma*," in *Nihonjin to ma*, Kenmochi Takehiko, ed., Kodansha, Tokyo 1981.

ma: the realm of society

Japanese collective conditioning is very well developed. The importance of sense of place to this mindset is revealed in some of the phrases used to describe cases of deficiency.

間抜け (*ma-nuke*)
Simpleton, fool (literally: someone missing ma)

間違う (*ma-chigau*)
To be mistaken (literally: place differs)

Clearly, the Japanese language is shot through with a dynamic sense of place. But the importance of the ma concept in society is best revealed in the everyday terms for "human being" and "the world":

人間 (*nin-gen*)
Human being (lit.: person-place or person-in-relationship)

世間 (*se-ken*)
World, society (literally: world-place or world-in-relationship)

仲間 (*naka-ma*)
Coterie; companion (literally: relationship-place)

Two related conclusions seems to offer themselves. First, that people are thought to exist only in the context of "place." Mankind was seen as only one component in a bigger whole of man/environment/nature. The implication is that the greater whole, rather than human beings by themselves, is the measure of all things. This is reinforced by Buddhist philosophy.

The second point is more obvious in Japanese behavior: everyone must have a social "place," for it is one's social relations, not one's individual characteristics, that constitute identity. Hence the ubiquitous name card, identifying the bearer's place and role. Traditionally, Japanese had no word corresponding to "individual" in the Western sense. The current word for "individual," *kojin* (個人, literally: item-person), was coined recently to express an imported Western notion. There has always been the common word for person/people, *hito* (人), but it refers to a discrete body and has none of the isolating nuance of the Western "individual."

In the Japanese language, and thus in the society, a person is conceived of as a flexible and easily linkable *dividuum*, that is, as part split from and belonging to a larger whole. Everyone is educated to shake off the delusion of a separate individual ego, and to express supra-individual values. What characterizes a person as human is that one is always together with other humans. In Japanese history, the only physical escape from the community was through withdrawal into the mountains, and in that case a person was referred to as *sen-nin* (仙人) "hermit," a word of otherworldly nuance. There never has been a Japanese word for "privacy."

In contrast, the Western mind has tended to envisage the human being as a perfect and self-contained *individuum* (that is, indivisible whole) who should be educated to distinguish themself from everyone else. We are encouraged to view the self as real, to discipline it and to express highly individual values. The desire to produce individual genius, a "superman," has haunted all of Western history.

The corresponding social ideals are of course diametrically opposed: the Western society of self-assertion, of the eternal conflict of individual interests; and the Japanese society of self-abnegation and harmony, of identity with the group, of common purpose.

In summary, ma in the subjective domain serves as an excellent unifying concept for Japanese awareness of *polarity*, of the yin-yang interaction of "opposites." There are the polarities of form and non-form (e.g. calligraphy and painting); of object and space (the house and its garden); of sound and silence, action and non-action, movement and rest (the performing arts); and of person and society.

Another way of looking at this sense of place or placement is in terms of the *continuum* that links the world into a single seamless structure. The concept of ma in the objective environment expresses the continuity of space and time, the time-structuring of space and the space-structuring of time. Ma in the subjective realm defines the continuum of event and experience, of external reality and internal mood.

One wonders what course Western philosophy would have taken if in any Western language a common denominator had existed between distance, area, space, time, person and world.

THE DOMAIN OF METAPHYSICS

Ma was adopted by Japanese Buddhists to express the notion of emptiness or the void. Two examples of this use by the poet-monk Saigyo in the twelfth century employ the following compound:

絶え間 (*taema*)
Pause, gap (literally: discontinuous place)

The first poem catches a momentary glance over the Inland Sea:

Kumori naki	Not clouded
yama nite umi no	mountains around the sea
tsuki mireba	in which the moon I see;
shima zo kohori no	the islands, in ice
tae-ma narikeri	holes become.

The second poem describes a rainstorm in the monk's hut:

mizu no oto wa	Sound of water,
sabishiki io no	of this lonely hermitage
tomo nare ya	the only friend becomes,
mine no arashi no	in the gaps and gaps
tae-ma tae-ma ni	of the mountain storm.[12]

12. LaFleur, William, "Saigyo and the Buddhist Value of Nature," Part II, *History of Religions*, Feb. 1974. The translations are my own.

The adoption of *taema* in these poems is an allusion to the Buddhist experience of *ku* (空), of the void or emptiness; the first uses a spatial metaphor, the second a temporal one. They are expressions not only a poet, but of a meditator too.

With the discussion of the void we have left the scope of phenomenology, architectural or otherwise. The "void" in the Buddhist sense is not a concept arrived at by rational thought, but an expression of an incommunicable individual experience, accessible only to a person practicing meditation.

The classic expression of the paradoxical nature of this emptiness or no-thingness is the *Heart Sutra*. It is one of the discourses ascribed to Gautama Buddha, and is recited by almost all Buddhist sects in Japan. It begins with:

> *Here, o Sariputra, form is emptiness and the very emptiness is form; emptiness does not differ from form, form does not differ from emptiness.*[13]

This world view offered by Buddhism only makes sense if one appreciates the first word of the sutra, the word "here." "Here" means "in my state of being," that is, enlightenment. Thus, for the normal human being the sutra cannot make sense; it will stay utterly paradoxical. Ultimately, nothing can be stated about the "void." It is impossible even to think about it.

Nevertheless, enlightened ones, each in their own way, have created many devices with which they have tried to lure their disciples into a state of being in which the above phrase does make sense.

Buddha used words, and what he said has been transmitted to us in the sutras. Chinese and Japanese enlightened masters who have followed his path have used poetry, painting and gardening to communicate their messages. One of the most famous examples, and for me an effective one, is the rock-garden at Ryoanji, the "Peaceful Dragon Temple" in Kyoto. We do not know who created the garden, nor when it was created in its present form.

13. Rajneesh, Bhagwan Shree, *The Heart Sutra*, Rajneesh Foundation, Poona, 1977.

It is a *karesansui* (dry landscape garden), to be appreciated from a fixed vantage point, on the veranda of the temple.

My suspicion is that the origin of the garden lies in meditation techniques using staring.[14] For here, the *object*—the natural rocks—is aesthetically so perfectly arranged in *space* — the finely raked white sand surface—that eventually the onlooker ceases to be aware of either the one or the other separately. The flow of energy is reversed and one is thrown onto the experience *per se*—consciousness.

This "experience"—the word has to be used in quotation marks now—of consciousness is the "experience" of the "void," of "no-thingness," of "emptiness." It is therefore not a philosophical or aesthetic concept, but a notion derived from personal experience, a notion both beside and beyond the experience of our physical world. It does not deny it. It is based on the reversal of the usual flow of our energy.

A blank surface of sand in front of a Buddhist temple or an empty sheet of white paper in Zen painting is not enough to trigger this insight. Architecture, gardening, painting or poetry, that is, some highly sophisticated setting of form and non-form, is necessary to "experience" the void in the above sense. Only a poet can put this paradox into words:

> *I dived down into the depth of the ocean of forms,*
> *hoping to gain the perfect pearl of the formless.*[15]

14. An outstanding explanation of visual meditation techniques is in Rajneesh, Bhagwan Shree, *The Book of Secrets, Vol. 2*, Rajneesh Foundation, Poona,1975, pp. 105–181
15. Tagore, Rabindranath, Poem 100, *Gitanjali*, London, 1914.

Illustration by Alex Mankiewicz

the unspoken space we share

by Pico Iyer

"I wonder if you might . . ."
"Mm . . ."
"It's a little difficult, perhaps . . . ?"
"Maybe . . ."
"Of course. We'll leave it till another time."

I never guessed, until I arrived in Japan, how much every exchange could be a dance—a duet of sorts—in which two people meet in the space between them. That a sentence can be a mere opening, for another person to extend, and so every conversation becomes a collaboration. It's not about you or me, deep down, but what we can do together.

A pen-and-ink drawing is an outline, only, that the viewer completes inside herself; a haiku is a prompt, a suggestion that allows you to bring the scene within. It's deeply personal, but it has nothing to do with personality; it's full of feeling, but the feeling belongs not to the first person singular, but plural.

A poet writes of spring rain on an empty path and you're on that path, feeling the precipitation upon your face; nothing comes between you and the scene that the poet has offered, least of all the poet himself. A haiku, like a thank you, is far too deep for "I."

In Japan I came to see that all our conversations might be like this, conspiracies. The monologue is not a form I encounter often on the streets of Kyoto, and, as in a haiku, the sentences I hear in Nara don't leave much room for argument or debate. They end in "*ne?*" ("right?") to beckon one into the exchange; they're directed in a way—"*desho*?" ("don't you think?")—that encourages affirmation and so communion.

I learned some of this growing up in England, where comments are softened and turned into questions so as not to be an intrusion: *"Might it be a little better, perhaps, if we thought of placing that sofa—and that assertion—over here?"* But in England such obliqueness can be a way of protecting privacy and reserve; in Japan it's more a way of bringing us out onto the common ground that is the larger self, the Whole.

In the foundational work of Japanese literature *The Tale of Genji*, according to the historian Ivan Morris, it's often hard to tell whether a statement is a question or not. Whether it's been delivered by a man or a woman. Even whether it's positive or negative. In everyday conversations in Japan today, pronouns are left out of the majority of sentences so that a declaration belongs not to me or you, but to the space we share.

For a writer, such delicacy is pure liberation: I know every sentence I commit will come to life only in someone else's head, if at all. My job is to offer a prompt that can become a world for somebody I'll never meet. Writing is often about the unspoken, of course—a pointing toward all that can't be said—but it's also an exercise in intimacy and connectedness. The less I impose of myself, the more the reader can make it her own.

I think of two of the most cherished haiku in Japan. Basho's celebration of the beautiful island of Matsushima takes the form of three lines in which he effectively just repeats the name of the island again and again; the beauty has stripped him of all words. There is nothing he can say that can surpass the wonder of what he sees. The world will always be richer than anything we can say of it.

And Issa's heartbroken haiku after the death of a child: "This world of dew is a world of dew, and yet . . ."

It hit me, soon after I touched down in Japan, that my neighbors speak much less than in other countries; the Japanese economy is at heart one of words and expressions. And when they do speak, my friends here often use the same words, in exactly the same cadences, so as not to complicate or smudge the exchange with the blur of personality. I made all kinds of withering assumptions when first I encountered this, until I realized it's a way of making discourse communal, and beyond the reach of tiny, mortal selves.

The pause, the murmur, the silence and the nod: these are the components of my conversations here. All ways of ushering us into the space between—and of schooling us in listening and hearing what lies between simplicities and conclusions. Buddhism tells us that the self doesn't exist and doesn't not exist; in Zen practice, the first koan is often *mu*—a kind of cousin to *ma*—which is sometimes said to mean "not one, not many, not no, not yes."

What a welcoming space that is, with room enough for mystery and what's bottomless, as well as for the few things we can know or say. I learned, after I'd begun to spend time in Kyoto, to say "I wonder" more than "I think." Maybe because, as Emily Dickinson, great mistresses of silences, has it:

Wonder—is not precisely Knowing
And not precisely Knowing not—

The space between is larger than you or I could ever be, and it will be here long after you and I are gone. Perhaps it's the shrine or temple before which every sentence might bow.

International House Garden, Tokyo, by Stephen Mansfield

some gravel, some stones

nature, art, and spirit in Japanese gardens

Stephen Mansfield interviews novelist Marion Poschmann

Marion Poschmann's novel *The Pine Islands*, set in Japan, was translated into English in 2019. Winner of the Berlin Prize for Literature, it was shortlisted for the Man Booker International Prize. The following are extracts from a discussion between the author, who is also a poet, and the Japan-based writer and photographer Stephen Mansfield, based on Marion Poschmann's three-month stay as a guest at Kyoto's Goethe-Institute Villa Kamogawa.

MANSFIELD: *I understand that a great deal of your time in Kyoto was spent in the city's gardens. What drew you to them? And how did you approach them?*

POSCHMANN: For many years I have been interested in the art of gardening. All the specific connotations, the Garden of Eden, paradise, the Arcadian landscape, you can find in a Baroque garden and as well in an English garden. When I visit a city, I always try at first to find the gardens and parks. I did so, for example, when I was spending a month in Kaliningrad. This was especially interesting, because there you can find parks originating from several times and ideological concepts: former German city parks, based on the opening of aristocratic gardens to the public; botanical and zoological gardens; typical Soviet parks with playgrounds; amusement parks; and parade grounds for the annual Victory Day marches. I found that you learn a lot about a country and its history by strolling through the gardens. And that was my intention when I was in Kyoto: to get in touch with Japanese aesthetics by visiting the Japanese gardens, to perceive their beauty, to contemplate them. And, of course, I read a lot about them, because usually you only see what you know.

You devote over a page of your novel, The Pine Islands, to an extensive listing of the varietals of the Japanese pine. Can you explain the centrality of the tree in your mind?

In one sense, my novel is a book mostly about trees. It deals with the Japanese pine and the American sugar maple, and my first idea was to write a book just about the beauty of these trees, a very quiet, meditative, poetical book. Actually, I started with a poem, which has the same title, "The Pine Islands." But a tree is not only beauty and nature, it represents history and politics, it is a symbol and a concept, and it was very interesting for me to compare how different countries look at their trees, which means looking in a way at themselves. The Japanese black pine is a tree connected with wisdom and strength and discipline. It is formally trimmed in a way that looks absolutely wild, so nature is formed into an image of nature, an idea of nature. In writing about pines, I wrote a book about projections and prejudices, culture and representation, traditions and modern society, dream and reality.

Another inspiration for the book came from Noh plays. I am fascinated by the structure of these plays, especially by the aspect of illusion. Most Noh dramas are a kind of ghost story, but you never know who plays the role of the ghost: the living person or the dead.

I wanted to do something similar, and I think my character Yosa fits in this scheme; he might be called a doppelgänger.

The descriptive passages in the book ring true. You must have spent time in Japan, researching settings?

I had the opportunity to spend three months in Kyoto during a residency at the Goethe Institute. I wanted to do research on Japanese aesthetics, I was fascinated by the specific Japanese arts like tea ceremony, ikebana, Noh, Kabuki, Butoh, and for the short time I had there I found it to be the most practicable way to concentrate on the Japanese garden. For three months, I visited the gardens of Kyoto, staring at stones and gravel, walking around ponds. This was a physical and a mental experience, similar to the pilgrimage my characters are on in the novel. It enhanced my sense of the differences between Eastern and Western aesthetic principles, for example asymmetry; the importance of shadows in contrast to Western culture stressing visibility; or of simplicity, based on incredibly complex rules. And one of my questions was, how do these principles survive in postmodern times?

Two years later I went back to Japan to see some places on the Basho route, during the *koyo* season of autumn leaves. I loved the idea of writing poetry at stations where so many other poets have looked at a particular landscape.

However, my text was almost finished, [I found] it feeds itself more from literature and imagination than from concrete perception. Strangely enough, my experience is that descriptions seem particularly realistic when they are constructed rather than mimetic.

Writers often talk about Japanese gardens replicating nature. It seems to me that the most accomplished landscapes go a step further by, not imitating nature, but transcending it. Would you agree?

I would absolutely agree. In the Japanese garden, there is no imitation of nature in the sense of wilderness. What might be replicated, is the idea of natural order, the image of spiritual sensitivity. In the Western tradition, the formal garden, for example Versailles, represents a cosmical order with its strict lines and flower beds and perspectives from one central point out into the open. The Japanese garden looks totally different, but the principle is similar, to create a surrounding which reminds us, for example, of the Islands of the Blessed, the Land of the Immortals. And because we do not know exactly, how these landscapes really look, it is important to create an atmosphere which calms the mind, which helps the mind to rise up.

It seems to me that in the dry landscape garden and the stroll garden we find dual, almost opposing urges in the Japanese mind. The former, simple, even humble, spiritually driven; the latter, beautiful but occasionally bordering on the ostentatious, a pleasure-driven entity. The temple and the amusement park.

The dry landscape garden and the stroll garden seem very different, they have different historical roots: the dry landscape garden being used for meditation in the temple, the monastery; the stroll garden for pleasure of the aristocratic class, for parties, boat trips, maybe with the hidden idea in the background to already belong to the group of immortals. In the tea garden, both aspects come together. You stroll around, you admire the moss and the gravel, you are either host or guest, that means, you are not alone, you are socializing, but the aim of such a meeting is not only to drink tea and chat a bit, but to enhance your own awareness.

Can you tell me a little about the themes contained in your yet-to-be translated essays on Japanese gardens?

The collection of my essays is not only about Japanese gardens, they deal with aesthetics and perception in many facets, but I wrote some pieces on Japanese themes: Ryoanji and my personal experiences there, the moon-viewing architecture, which fascinates me especially as a poet, because the moon is one of the most important motifs in traditional poetry, but I never had heard of special devices to view the moon before: a terrace near a pond, in order to see the moon mirrored in the water, or a little tower with a round, moonlike window, I found it just incredible. In German, my essays are called *Mondbetrachtung in mondloser Nacht*, that might be translated as "Moon Viewing on a Moonless Night," and this title hints at the power of imagination. Another essay tells about my visit to the garden of Saiho-ji or Koke-dera, the famous moss garden in Kyoto, and there I reflect on the taxonomic differences, the biological difficulties to distinguish a hundred species of moss—it is said that in Koke-dera you find a hundred varieties of mosses. And this raises both linguistic and poetic questions, because who knows a hundred different mosses?

Lafcadio Hearn wrote about Japanese gardens, that they were "gardens of the past. The future will know them only as dreams, creations of a forgotten art." Do you sense the decline of contemporary gardens created in the spirit of the past?

The stunning effect of the traditional Japanese gardens is that they seem absolutely modern. At least in comparison with European or in general Western gardens, the asymmetry of the stone settings looks like they were positioned randomly, but there is a system, only you cannot grasp it with logical efforts. In this sense, it might be the case that a contemporary garden, constructed in the spirit of the past, is more or less a copy and maybe lacks depth. But my experience is that the contemporary gardens I have seen achieve a new kind of depth in their own way. In Germany, I recently saw a building created by Japanese architect Tadao Ando. The Langen Foundation is a museum of modern art, built on the grounds of a former NATO rocket base, and it is surrounded by a garden made of concrete walls, a water basin and a row of Japanese cherry trees. This garden is really different from a formal garden, but I think it transports the spirit of the past and also includes the remembrance of events which have happened in recent decades, especially in Germany.

Shigemori Mirei Garden Museum (Kyoto), by Stephen Mansfield.

Is there a risk, then, that formal gardens, even those engorged with living plants, may become mummified cultural artifacts?

I don't feel it like that; on the contrary, those places are much more vivid than other artifacts and also than other cultural spaces. The construction is in a way timeless, and the people visiting these gardens every day are enriching them with their mode of perception. And such a formal garden is not just standing there over the centuries—every day it demands a certain maintenance, like raking, weeding, or washing the dust from the stones. One can call it a procedure which revives the garden again and again.

Zen writer Alan Watts contended that the creator of a dry landscape garden possesses no "mind to impose his own intention upon natural forms, but is careful rather to follow the 'intentionless intention' of the forms themselves." Do you think contemporary garden designers have the requisite sensitivity to achieve that state of mind?

As I know it, regular meditation is a kind of basic exercise to achieve such a state of mind and to create, in a second step, a garden. Each garden might mirror the state of mind of its creator. I see no reason why a contemporary designer should not be able to follow the "intentionless intention" of the form itself. What excited me, when I was reading old Japanese garden manuals, was the idea that in Shintoism the stones are looked at as living beings. So, the garden designer has to fulfill the wish of the main stone, and then react to the wishes of the other stones. I wonder if these conceptions are still accepted in contemporary garden design.

I think they are. The garden designer and Zen priest, Shunmyo Masuno, talks about listening to the "request" of stones, contending that one should "converse" with them, waiting "until they seem to speak and say where they want to be placed." Is it fair to say that experiencing the Japanese garden enables us to examine other arts and practices, fine-tunes taste,

enhances our appreciation of Japanese aesthetics, and develops a kind of connoisseurship of our critical faculties?

I have to admit that I know several people who have seen Japanese gardens and found them nothing but boring. My personal experience is that you need some time to tune into the mood of these gardens, to be able to endure the silence and to tolerate the subtleties. In our daily life, we are not used to such surroundings, and after some weeks in the Japanese gardens I observed that other visitors became often quite nervous, they immediately took some photographs and avoided staying there any longer. The thing is, experiencing the Japanese garden challenges the whole person, one has to change oneself first, and only then are you yourself fine, refined enough, to appreciate their finenesses.

Japanese aesthetics, in this instance, those applied to gardens, can seem quite unfathomable at first. Concepts like* seijaku *(absolute stillness),* koko *(precious simplicity), and* yugen *(profound depth and beauty), are not easily grasped. How did you approach these ideas?

These concepts were unfamiliar to me, or at least I didn't know the terms. My impression was that Western aesthetics do not seem that differentiated, I could not tell that we have an equivalent to yugen or koko. But nevertheless, these ideas felt somehow natural to me—as an artist I deal with them, even if I do not name them. It was a great relief for me to realize that one can communicate conceptually about these matters, even though they are very subtle things that are difficult to express.

Gardening principles imply a collaboration between the natural and the contrived. Given this deliberate creative process, the filtration of natural elements into preconceived forms, does that mean that the most accomplished gardens can be considered as works of art? Mara Miller, for example, an Asian Studies specialist, has called the Japanese garden a "subspecies of visual art," a form of virtual space . . .

Of course, they are works of art, they create a visual space and also, what is much more important, a mental space. For me it is most interesting that in Japanese gardens you do not have to decide if it is a work of nature or a work of art, because in contrast to Western aesthetics these concepts are not divided. I found it fascinating, that a Japanese garden unites nature, art and also spirituality. The artistic character is only one aspect, or maybe this specific type of artwork is nourished by the beauty of nature and the boundlessness of the mind, so that you become aware not only of the outer, but also of the inner space you usually don't notice.

The eighteenth century English landscape designer, Humphrey Repton, wrote that "one of the fundamental principles of landscape gardening is to disguise the real boundary." Might this be interpreted to mean that the garden is, in fact, confined, but, at least in the imagination of the viewer, limitless?

The poetry collection I wrote during my residence in Japan has the title *Borrowed Landscapes*. This is a term taken from the art of gardening, and it means that the construction of the garden includes elements which are located outside of the walls, for example a mountain or a pagoda. In Kyoto you find several gardens where the trees or hedges are arranged in a way that it seems as if the garden extends far into the landscape. One of the most famous examples is the imperial garden of Shugaku-in Rikyu. It operates with surprising effects. You walk through a labyrinth of hedges up to the top of a hill, and suddenly the view opens over the whole valley. In the Chinese garden manual *Yuan Ye* from 1631, the garden architect Ji Cheng describes for the first time the technique of borrowed landscape: it is important to evoke even in a limited space all the power and vastness of nature. And in my experience, this often succeeds.

In the Japanese garden, as in other disciplines like ceramic making, a defect might be considered an effect. One recalls Leonard Cohen's lyric: "There is a crack, a crack in everything. That's how the light gets in."

Were the merits of imperfection something that you noticed during your Kyoto garden immersion?

I know that imperfection is one of the major traits in Japanese aesthetics, but honestly speaking, I consider the effects of imperfection much more obvious in ceramics than in gardens. A broken tea bowl is repaired with gold and lacquer, so the crack becomes an ornament. A garden is always changing, the light is different each hour, the plants are growing, losing their leaves and so on. In a garden, there is never a state of perfection reached, something is always lacking, you have either the blossoms or the snow or the turning leaves. But if perfection is meant to be symmetry—yes, I noticed, that there is no symmetry in a Japanese garden, the sense of harmony is absolutely different in comparison to a garden of symmetry. Asymmetric patterns keep you awake, they show you, that every moment, every view is always new.

You mentioned the landscape designer Shigemori Mirei once. He's quite a divisive figure in the gardening world, some characterizing him as creative iconoclast, others as despoiler of traditions. What's your take on the man?

As I know it, Shigemori Mirei adapted influences of Western art and introduced them in his garden design. He studied the Surrealists, and some of his stone settings look really wild and emotional, as if they might bring up patterns of the unconscious. I really admire his work, I think it is a convincing renewal of the traditional garden, although it does not transmit the same calmness. It is a work of our time, and maybe it helps us to appreciate the features of the traditional gardens even more.

Japanese gardens might be said to inspire a sense of refined introspection. Was that your experience?

My experience was that all the traditional Japanese art disciplines deepen that refined introspection. The visitor of a garden is always led from the everyday world into a world of the mind. Personally, I was sometimes overwhelmed by the power and the stillness when I came to a garden and expected nothing special. I do not dare to say if this stillness comes from the garden or from one's own mind. In reality, there is nothing spectacular to see: some gravel, some stones.

Zen tells us that stillness is a prerequisite in attaining peace of mind, and yet the world is in perpetual, restless motion. Is it possible that the Japanese garden, in its mastery of space, its transmuting of nature into art, can provide that stillness?

The Japanese garden can of course provide this stillness, but even more, it can also help to find this stillness outside. I believe you can experience it in a parking lot, if you only once felt it concentrated and refined in a formal garden. In a garden, of course, it is easier.

I wrote in one of my books that, "Gardens may not change our life, but they can improve it immeasurably." How did your time among the gardens of Kyoto effect you?

It is maybe not that exaggerated to say it changed my life, because it really opened a new world for me, or at least a new view of the world. It was fantastic to learn that in Japan, subtle beauty has such an importance, the background, the empty spaces, the shadows, the invisible. I don't dare to say that I could have acquired even the basics of this aesthetic, but I have found something in it that comes very close to my own intentions, without having been able to verbalize beforehand what I was actually looking for.

Shisen-do, by Allan Mandell

invitations to stillness

Japanese gardens as metaphorical journeys of solace

by Mark Hovane

In his essay "Of Gardens" published in 1625, Francis Bacon wrote:

> God Almighty planted a garden and indeed, it is the purest of human pleasures; it is the greatest refreshment to the spirits of man.

The garden is arguably more relevant and essential today than ever before. We live in a globalized world of instant gratification and season-less possibilities. Environmental destruction and climate change proceed at an unprecedented rate. We are disorientated and detached from the natural order of things. In our technology-obsessed world, our connection with natural places has become even more imperative to our mental and physical equilibrium as individuals, communities and society as a whole. There is a significant and growing body of research documenting the power of nature to heal and relax us, restoring physical, cognitive and emotional balance.

Humans created gardens to condense the beauty of nature into a limited space which could easily be accessed as part of everyday life. Gardens contain nature but the distressing and challenging elements are removed. Furthermore, a garden is raw nature tamed and shaped by the human hand. German architect and garden scholar Gunter Nitschke contends:

> The garden could be said to stand at the crossroads of nature and culture, of matter and consciousness. It is neither one nor the other; it discloses both in the form of human art.[1]

Renaissance humanist Sir Thomas More said:

> The many great gardens of the world, of literature and poetry, of painting and music, of religion and architecture, all make the point as clear as possible: the soul cannot thrive in the absence of a garden. If you don't want paradise you are not human, and if you are not human you don't have a soul.

The idea of a "healing garden" is both ancient and modern. The term "therapeutic landscape" has recently come to the forefront of the field of landscape architecture, however these "restorative spaces" are not new concepts and have in fact been implemented for millennia. Persian gardens dating back to the sixth century BC helped connect individuals with Deity and heavenly glory. They were spaces designed to provide rest and encourage contemplation. Similarly restorative spaces were evident in medieval European monastery cloisters as well as Japanese Zen temples.

Japanese gardens in general have long had religious underpinnings from both the indigenous Shinto belief system as well as from the later cultural import of Buddhism. Sacred, otherworldly and extraordinary, they were even written about in *The Chronicles of Japan,* the second-oldest book of Japanese history, compiled in the year 720. Traditionally, the Japanese believed that natural elements of nature were manifestations of spirits called *kami,* thought to reside in mountains, rivers, trees and stones. Later, as Zen Buddhism from China took hold in the twelfth

1. Gunter Nitschke. *Japanese Gardens* (Taschen, 1999)

Toji-in, by Allan Mandell

century, many gardens were constructed within temple precincts to provide spaces for contemplation, far from the stresses of the secular world. Their aim was to reduce the elements of nature to symbolic representation for a minimalist essence. Zen is based on the practice of seated meditation as a core spiritual discipline with the aim of connecting the individual to the larger cosmos. These gardens helped people escape worldly afflictions and strengthen spiritual resolve.

The practice of garden-making in Japan has a long history and, over the last 1500 years, there have been many changes in perceptions of what constitutes a garden. Although Japanese gardens have been influenced and inspired by the introduction of new religions and philosophies, we can surmise that there has always been a spiritual dimension to Japanese landscaped space.

As transformative healing spaces, the most relevant Japanese gardens are those which have their origins in medieval Japan. Influenced by Zen philosophy, dry landscape *karesansui* gardens were usually located in Zen temples, typically featuring white sand or gravel to metaphorically represent the element of water. Larger stones placed within this expanse of raked ground represented mountains. These gardens were completed with minimal vegetal

Kennin-ji by Allan Mandell

material. The other highly symbolic, contemplative spaces were tea gardens, *roji*, which developed toward the end of the sixteenth century, usually surrounding a tea house or hut, designed to prepare the guests spiritually as they moved slowly toward the tea event. Later, small courtyard gardens, *tsuboniwa*, appeared in merchant townhouses to represent a condensed version of a tea garden. The raison d'être of each of these different types of garden was to focus attention inward. Thus it can be seen that only with the rise of Zen in medieval Japan did gardens become so deliberately symbolic of the human quest for inner understanding. From these historical principles, it becomes clear that Japanese gardens are potent opportunities for self-realization, tranquility and peace. Buddhism has investigated the garden as a tool for religious teaching, practice and contemplation for centuries. Garden maker and twelfth-century Zen priest Muso Kokushi observed:

> He who distinguishes between the garden and practice cannot be said to have found the Way.

In Japan, the act of tending a garden is also a form of Buddhist practice, implying commitment to nurturing a daily habit that cultivates inner healing and spiritual growth. The garden invites humility and rewards patient maintenance. In fact the meticulous care required of a Japanese garden in particular, distinguishes it from many other cultures' landscaped spaces. Partly this is a response to the limited physical space that necessitates a delicate balance of scaled relationships between garden elements. It is a well known rule for traditional gardeners that a great garden relies 40 percent on design and 60 percent on maintenance. Every element in the Japanese garden, from the shape of the pruned pine trees to the careful placement of stepping stones, has intention and is specifically designed to cultivate nuanced awareness. The contrast between what is placed and what is left blank brings to life a pictorial space that leaves room for our imagination. Symbolism and metaphor in the garden also offer powerful tools to help humans reconcile their own lives and relationships to both society and the larger forces of nature. American garden scholar Kendall Brown argues:

> The opportunity for direct engagement with nature is what makes all gardens compelling but, as Japanese gardens function so effectively as philosophical and physical microcosms, their power is even stronger.[2]

Modernist architect and theorist Garrett Eckbo says:

> Japanese gardens are probably the most highly refined and completely developed garden conceptions our world culture has known. They are perfectly suited as spaces for withdrawal, repose and as places where one seeks order in a disorderly world.[3]

Japanese gardens employ centuries of wisdom about sensory and cognitive experience of space and nature's inherent energies. Sophisticated spatial modulation is one of the defining characteristics of Japanese landscaped space. Central as a design technique is the concept of *ma*, a very complex idea that permeates almost every

2. Kendall Brown. *Visionary Landscapes* (Tuttle, 2017)
3. Garrett Eckbo in Kendall Brown, *Visionary Landscapes* (Tuttle, 2017)

aspect of Japanese culture. The word ma has no literal translation but can be referred to as space, place or void. Ma can be expressed spatially, temporally, socially and as a combination of any of these. The manipulation of ma is one of the most compelling and complex aspects of the Japanese garden. As a positive design element, it also has a precedent in Chinese landscape painting. Empty space enlivens and potentiates the objects it resides between, leading to a dynamic tension that is paradoxically calming. It creates an opportunity in the imagination of the human mind that experiences these elements to enter the field and complete the work of art. A sense of place emerges with an emphasis on interval that creates a simultaneous awareness of form and non-form. In assessing a garden's design, renowned contemporary garden designer and Zen Buddhist priest Shunmyo Masuno asks:

> Has the space in the garden been properly attended to? Is the overall atmosphere one of harmony and yet harmony which still possesses a "robust tension?"[4]

It is the pared-down tension between the garden's elements that contributes to the healing energy of the garden. To get philosophical, the inclusion of the formless, of eternity, of nothingness is what gives great art depth. Zen scholar Shinichi Hisamatsu has described this requirement for the inclusion of "background" or "depth" in Japanese art as "subtle profundity" or "deep reserve."[5] The result of this profundity is an inexhaustibility which allows the viewer to come back to the work of art again and again and each time be rewarded with a freshness which reveals another aspect which had not been appreciated before.

Over centuries, the techniques of Japanese garden design were developed to direct one's experience in subtle but specific ways; to lessen preoccupation with the self and foster an increased awareness

4. Shunmyo Masuno. "Landscapes in the Spirit of Zen: A Collection of the Work of Shunmyo Masuno". (*Process Architecture*, 1995)
5. Shinichi Hisamatsu. *Zen and the Fine Arts*, trans. G. Tokiwa (Kodansha International, 1982)

of nature and our relation to it. Japanese gardens have ma that is physical, visual and temporal. Above all, ma must be felt viscerally. Ma should be an experience that energizes our whole being. When this occurs, we are experiencing a space that cannot be measured. What results is the freedom of an imaginative space that we as visitors co-create in the garden. Using an analogy from Japanese tea ceremony: if the garden acts as "host," it is clear that ma extends an invitation to the visitor as "guest" to accept the "hospitality" of the garden as a work of art. There is an etiquette to being a good guest. A viewer must acquire a proper attitude for viewing.

There is a deliberate order and conduct necessary to fully experience the Japanese garden as an immersive artwork in progress. Exquisitely choreographed pathways, gates and water features are all consciously designed to slow the visitor down, allowing a divesting of the outside world to encounter timeless space. Japanese gardens need time to work their magic and draw the visitor in. A Japanese garden is a sensitively managed visual environment, with the visitor's experience at the center. A fundamental design concern has always been the question of how the visitor will interact with the space.

This way in which the garden engages the visitor is one of the key elements that distinguishes it as a healing space. When asked for advice on how to view a Japanese garden, another twentieth-century garden master Kinsaku Nakane answered: "With a detached gaze and in a state of total receptivity."[6]

A garden is an invitation to aesthetic, mental and sensory experience. As visitors, we cannot DO a garden, we must BE in it.

For a garden to make effective use of limited space, the visitor needs to be drawn into the garden and become part of the experience as a whole. As one enters the garden, there is a break with everyday life and the beginning of a multidimensional landscape of possibilities, as though we were given new eyes with which to see the world. An old Zen teaching posits that we start to "see with our

6. David A. Slawson. *Secret Teachings in the Art of Japanese Gardens* (Kodansha International, 1987)

ears and listen with our eyes." Being in the garden for an extended period, we start to notice the nuanced green palette of the plants. The dappled patterns of sunlight for which the Japanese ascribe the poetic word *komorebi* creates a chiaroscuro-like dark brightness. The garden's silence heightens each and every sound. We are lifted out of the mundane into a heightened reality. One is not only in the garden but now a part of it, a visitor no more. A merging of the self with nature. To feel at one with the garden is to become the garden. Japanese philosopher Kitaro Nishida (1870–1945) describes Japanese culture's most characteristic feature as moving from subject to object:

> To say that we know a thing simply means that the self unites with it. When one sees a flower, the self has become the flower.[7]

What we see and take from the garden depends on ourselves, on our willingness to enter a space beyond beauty; our surrender allows us to see with our heart.

My circumambulation thus complete,
With fresh serenity I take my seat
Upon the veranda-step; in silence gaze
At stones and sand that shimmer in a haze
Of brightness through the sultry atmosphere;
Until their contemplation empties thought
And space becomes a calm and conscious blaze.
At once myself and garden disappear
Into its boundless circle, centered here
In evanescent beings, lightly buoyed
Like summer clouds amid the formless Void
Beyond duality: both infinite Nought,
And fifteen stones within a graveled court.[8]

7. Kitaro Nishida. "Intelligibility and the Philosophy of Nothingness: Three Philosophical Essays" in Robert E Carter, *The Japanese Arts and Self Cultivation* (SUNY Press, 2008)
8. Harold Stewart. *By the Old Walls of Kyoto* (Weatherhill, 1981)

a form of emptiness

ma in the tea ceremony

by Alexandre Avdulov and John McGee
drawings by Alec Brown

It has just rained, the drops cascading from leaf to leaf—one of those Kyoto rains that appears from nowhere and seems to freshen the whole universe. Now the sky is clear, visible through the carefully plucked pine needles that are thinned twice a year so the sky and the moon can be seen through them. Entering an opened gate lightly sprinkled with water, the guests find themselves in a *roji*—a tea garden which connects the gate and the waiting room to the arbor and the teahouse. No matter how physically small, it always gives a feeling of spaciousness, of a quiet, protected, comforting space, inviting you to pause and stay longer.

The path winding through the roji is called *tobiishi*—"scattered stones." Though carefully selected, leveled and combined, their positioning appears entirely natural. Framed by green moss, the stones are washed and dried with a white towel before each tea, then lightly sprinkled with water just before the guests arrive so when they step on the path it feels as if light rain has just fallen.

The stones are placed so you step comfortably from one to the next but you can't walk along looking up at the sky or thc trees;

your attention is brought to each step, slowed and focused by smaller stones. You cannot rush; you must pause and notice the space. The path is never simply a straight line, making it a meandering journey to arrive at the entrance. You take your time. An occasional larger stone encourages you to pause to look around. You notice the sound of wind in the trees above, the fresh smell of moist moss and the glint of light from dew on the ferns. Within minutes of passing through the gate you've embarked upon a solitary pilgrimage.

The sixteenth century tea master Sen no Rikyu took the term *roji* from a passage in the *Lotus Sutra* which mentions the dewy path separating our daily life from the world of the spirit, in this case, the teahouse. "*Chanoyu*, commonly known as the Japanese tea ceremony, is an interdisciplinary complex, a synthesis of traditional Japanese and world arts and crafts combined with multiple cultural elements and brought together in a creative ritual of preparing, making and sharing a bowl of tea. It nurtures unified awareness through the refinement of all six senses in harmony and tranquility. Unlike many other meditative practices, this happens without detachment from the real world with its colors, tastes, sounds, fragrances and textures." (Avdulov, *Listening to the Pines, in Silence and the Silenced*, Peter Lang Publishing, 2013.)

The guests have been invited to a *chaji*, a formal tea gathering for three to five guests, which is at the heart of chanoyu practice. The written invitation simply states: "I'd like to offer you a bowl of tea." Even though most tea students go to their teacher's tearoom weekly to learn the many forms of tea preparation, a chaji, which brings together all the elements of chanoyu, is a rare experience for them. And yet the chaji, a four-hour long ceremony encompassing two fire preparations, a meal and two types of tea preparation, is the guiding principle of chanoyu practice since it determines and sets all the parameters of the learning process. The bowl of tea offered to all the guests to share is called *koicha*, thick tea, the finest tea made from slowly ground leaves kneaded by a bamboo whisk. The other tea offered later is called *usucha*, thin tea, which will be familiar to anyone who has attended a *chakai*, a more informal gathering for larger numbers of guests, or simply had a bowl of matcha in a temple or restaurant. This tea is whisked and offered to each guest individually.

The shoji screen doors leading to the entrance area are slightly ajar, enough to slide your palm in to open them. In the *machiai* waiting room, guests observe a scroll, usually a seasonal ink painting, that in its abstractness and seeming lack of color depicts not only the form of objects but also transmits their very essence. The poetics of understatement and vagueness hint at rather than describe, activating the viewer's perception by luring them into the process of co-creation and the interpretation of what is not said or depicted. An asymmetrically placed image is balanced by the seemingly empty space which becomes the sphere for the active emotional participation of the viewer. A tiny image or even just a gradation of ink makes the seemingly empty space next to it look as if it were an eternal cosmos. This "effect of absence" is fundamental in chanoyu, and is an essential aspect of the principle of *ma*. Not only what is directly observed but also that which is not visually depicted but is felt has an equally strong impact. The "presence of absence" is as important as the presence of presence. Fifteenth century Zen painter Sesshu elevated the viewing angle on many ink paintings. The viewer observes his work as though on a platform looking at the scenes from a 45-degree angle. This angle is the view when using the washing basin, making tea and viewing the utensils.

The Noh actor Komparu Kunio writes that ma "can be translated into English as space, spacing, interval, gap, blank, room, pause, rest, time, timing, or opening . . . [it is] a unique conceptual term, one without parallel in other languages." (Komparu, *The Noh Theatre: Principles and Perspectives*, Weatherhill/Tankosha, 1983.) He says when the concept first came from China it only referred to space, but as it evolved in Japan it included time too. The fact that ma refers to space and to time makes it unique. But there is a third meaning of the term which is "space/time" where space and time

merge into one experience of the moment in space. Chanoyu gives a form to ma: it combines time, space and experience into one.

While waiting, the guests are offered a taste of warm water. This water, drawn at dawn from a well or a natural spring, is used for all elements of the chaji. The cups are warmed and filled to about one third so there is room for the steam to rise. The guests now proceed to an arbor in the garden. Open on one side it gives the seated guests a different view of the roji. From the arbor, the guests can hear the host pouring fresh water into the stone water basin to purify it, just out of sight. The host opens a low, loosely woven bamboo gate and sees the guests for the first time. All bow in silence. The guests go from the outer garden to the inner garden closer to the teahouse. Before entering, the guests squat to purify their hands and mouths at the *tsukubai*, a low stone washing basin.

The tsukubai is a group of rocks precisely placed in relation to each other. Each stone is selected for its function and balance with the others. The most important one is the largest, with an opening to be filled with water. A hidden space is scooped out under the perimeter so the round wooden ladle can enter easily to draw water. This opening is always made by hand, never by machine. The basin is carefully leveled so the water can reflect the moon or lantern light. Once the main rock is installed, the one you squat on is placed so one can reach the ladle and the water comfortably. On the left and right, smaller rocks are placed to be used for a hot-water bucket in winter and a candle for evening teas. The space before the basin rock is filled with pebbles with a small but distinctive rock placed in the center. This is called the Dragon Gate.

The space between the front rock and the main basin plus the "extension" formed by the ladle handle creates a pause, a chance to notice both space and time, the sky and surroundings. The roji is discovered gradually, carefully, mindfully, step by step. Reaching for water, glimpsing the water surface, then intentionally breaking it by scooping water with the ladle and creating a new water surface and bringing it close to oneself, once again seeing the mirror water and pouring it onto your palm, changing hands and creating another surface of water. This sequence creates mirrors of reflections, precision enveloped in space and pause, the essence of ma.

One by one the guests purify their hands and approach the tearoom. Its entrance is open just a little. The first guest slides open the small, square door, just big enough for one person to scrunch through, and looks inside. Though physically small, the space feels vast and enticing. The faint aroma of sandalwood, said to be the scent of the Buddha, welcomes. When the last guest has come in, the door is shut with a bang to let the host know everyone has entered. The room is empty except for a scroll in the *tokonoma* alcove and a brazier holding a wet kettle steaming as it dries on the charcoal fire. The light coming in through several small, papered windows is subdued, like dawn or twilight, said to be best for meditation. There is no view of the outside garden, only the natural muted colors of mud plaster walls, wooden and bamboo posts and the tatami mats. The ceiling is often more complex, with different levels, the highest above the guests' tatami and the lowest above the host's preparation mat.

The first guest sits in front of the tokonoma to face the scroll. The tokonoma alcove, recessed in one of the tearoom's walls, first became part of tearoom architecture in the sixteenth century, incorporating Zen temple altars into the secular tea house, reflecting the blending of the spiritual and aesthetic practice of Tea. The calligraphy on the scroll, often a Zen phrase brushed by a Zen monk or a tea master, is in essence a transmission of the world of spirit. Both Zen and Tea strive to seek eternity in a single moment in time. Often the calligraphy is so stylized as to be unreadable. But the energy of each stroke, the gradation of ink, and the flow of lines create a special vigor that the viewer connects to. This doesn't happen after careful inspection of the calligraphy but immediately, at first glance. It moves you not just intellectually through the meaning of the Zen phrase but also emotionally. It's just a moment, an individual, private, intimate moment, different for each guest, but the group is united by each having had this moment. As if based on its ideographic nature, the calligraphy evokes deep essential connections with painting. Here meaning and form, intellect and intuition coalesce in a single enlightening moment. A calligraphic character can possess aesthetic qualities independent from its meaning, letting it echo in a person's heart.

When you are in front of the scroll, you first make a deep bow, look at the calligraphy and the mounting of the scroll then make another deep bow. You face the scroll directly, protected by the walls of the tokonoma from all three sides, making this public moment private and intimate. The space and the specially designated time make this experience unique. The host will have chosen this scroll for this particular chaji and for this particular main guest. This experience is just a single moment, unrepeatable and indelible.

The "onceness" of Tea is reflected in the phrase *ichigo ichie.* Each meeting is a once-in-a-lifetime event. This phrase has become deeply associated with Tea since its introduction by Ii Naosuke, a nineteenth-century samurai tea man. *Ichigo* refers to a person's life from birth to death, something never to be repeated, while *ichie* is a coming together of people. Life is transient. Whoever you meet you will part from. Every meeting is unique and will never happen again in the same way. Tea is a way of encouraging the practitioner to focus attention on even the smallest details.

The host slides the door open, and everyone bows. So much in Tea is done in silence and with silence, so much is understood without words and orchestrated from within. The host is invited to slide in and after an exchange of greetings, the first guest, who does most of the talking and communication with the host, asks about the various objects that have been introduced so far. Gratitude and appreciation for this opportunity to share but a moment in time is conveyed through a highly structured dialogue, yet with plenty of improvisation. Knowing when to speak and when to keep silent is de rigueur in a chaji. The host and main guest carry on an erudite conversation, primed with mindfulness, thoughtfulness, humor, and a deep insight into the practice, informed by awareness of ma.

A simple kaiseki meal is offered before tea in a chaji. Sen no Rikyu, in one of his seven rules of chanoyu, said "food is enough if it satisfies hunger." Rikyu, a layman Zen practitioner, modified the protocols for eating in Zen temples for use in the tearoom. Just enough of the freshest ingredients, served simply and eaten quietly. The host brings in square black lacquer trays, each bearing two lidded lacquer bowls sprinkled with a fine "dew," and a ceramic dish on which fish is served. A moistened pair of fragrant cedar chopsticks rests on the edge of each tray. Rikyu's design of black trays, bowls, rice containers and hot water pitchers is still used today. Their classic simplicity has remained unsurpassed.

The first guest slides forward to receive their tray from the host, and both bow silently. When all guests have been served, the host asks everyone to pick up their chopsticks. In unison the guests take the lids off the bowls and place them to the side. In the left bowl is the first of three servings of rice, in the shape of the Japanese character signifying the word "one," a glistening white wedge steaming in the dark curve of the black lacquer. In the right bowl is a warm, ruddy miso soup containing a simmered round of daikon radish garnished with a dab of mustard. After the guests have tasted the rice and the soup, the host brings in a metal-handled sake container and a set of red-lacquered shallow sake cups on a black stand. Each guest is offered sake by the host and the guests then taste the fish, caught that morning.

Next, a round, lidded black lacquer container containing rice that will be shared is placed before the main guest. The lid of the rice container is passed hand to hand to the last guest. Each pause to admire the dew-like condensation from the warm rice on the lid. The host then brings in the main course, a clear broth soup made that morning from kelp and dried bonito flakes containing an assortment of fish, and carefully cut seasonal vegetables with an aromatic accent on top. The guests hold the large, elegantly decorated lacquer bowl and open the lid a crack to appreciate the aroma of the broth before putting down the lid and enjoying the fresh, subtly flavored ingredients. More sake, a charcoal-grilled dish and one more bowl of seasonal ingredients is brought in. The guests serve themselves rice, the offered dishes and sake. When finished, they pass around the empty bowls to admire. After removing the dishes, the host brings in small, lacquered bowls with a portion of pickled plum in broth, as a taste refresher. Then, delicacies from the sea and the mountain are brought in on a dampened cedar tray with green bamboo chopsticks along with more sake. The host serves one portion of ocean produce while offering each guest a cup of sake. The same procedure follows for the mountain produce, however this time the host receives sake from the guests.

Lastly, the host brings a lacquer pitcher holding crispy rice from the bottom of the rice pot and hot water on a tray with an assortment of lightly pickled fresh vegetables. The guests serve themselves and use the pickles to clean the lacquer bowls with the slightly salted warm water as was done in medieval Zen monasteries. A yellow pickled daikon radish, *takuan*, named after a seventeenth century Zen monk, Takuan Soho, who was fond of these pickles, is often served. (He even wrote a poem about them). At the end the guests drop their cedar chopsticks in unison on the lacquer tray. The host, hearing this sound, opens the door and takes the trays away. Next the host opens the door and bows with a bamboo basket of charcoal by their side to lay the fire to heat the water for tea.

Each charcoal piece is precisely cut to a certain size and is placed in a brazier from the largest to the smallest as if to offer the whole tree. The brazier holds an ash formation prepared only for this tea. The host prepares the finely powdered ash by smoothing and cutting the form with copper spoons using only the weight of the spoon, drawn with gentle but firm movements. To finish, white powdered ash is sprinkled over the precise shape of the ash. Taking off the kettle from the trivet, the ash looks like mountains and valleys appearing in the brazier. After all the charcoal pieces have been placed, a satisfying chirping sound signals that the charcoal is catching. The host opens a small incense container and places sandalwood incense chips on and near the charcoal, where it will be gently heated but not burnt. Almost immediately the fragrance permeates the whole room.

Next, guests are offered *okashi*, moist sweets. These are always freshly made for the gathering and always reflect a particular micro season. Okashi reminiscent of water are offered in summer to provide a feeling of coolness; ones suggesting warmth are served in winter. Their taste lingers during the interval and perfectly complements the taste of the tea that will be offered after the break. After the okashi, the guests once again look at the scroll and the brazier and go back to the arbor. Only a few hours have passed since their arrival but much has changed, both within and without. The capacity to notice, to observe and to feel has been heightened by the experience in the tearoom so the landscape of the garden looks somehow different. The light is different later in the day, of course, but it's mostly because the inner state of mind has expanded.

To call the guests back to the tearoom the host strikes a gong producing a deep, sonorous sound. At the first sound, all the guests leave their seats in the arbor and squat down the better to hear since such a deep sound travels close to the ground.

LOUD – soft – LOUD – soft – medium-medium – LOUD

Like many aspects of Tea, the way the gong is struck tells the listening guests of the years of practice the host has undergone. When the sound has faded, the first guest walks out of sight to the tsukubai washing basin to purify their hands and mouth and then to the tearoom. Each guest walks alone once again to reenter the tearoom. This time when they pause at the entrance, they hear the sound made by the simmering iron kettle, reminiscent of the sound of wind in the pines, a sound that has become a metaphor for chanoyu. Over the next half hour, the sound will grow stronger and become the background to the tea preparation. However, it is only heard when one takes time to sit quietly and listen.

When the guests reenter the tearoom, they proceed to the tokonoma again. The scroll has been taken down and replaced by flowers, called *chabana,* "flowers for tea," simply placed in a vase made of bamboo, ceramic or bronze. As Rikyu taught, the flowers are not arranged, they are simply placed facing the guests in a spacious and natural manner "as if growing in the field," the leaves

glistening with freshly sprinkled "dew." Tea masters of the past taught that in the tearoom pure flowers should be placed in pure water with a pure mind. That pure mind is a spacious, open mind, uncluttered by perceptions and the desire to self-express—a mind that will follow the lead of the flowers. Pure flowers are those about to open. The host has only a few moments to place the flowers, and their immediacy is transmitted to the guest in this unique and never-to-be-repeated moment. After looking at the flowers, the guests observe the brazier and the utensils brought in during the intermission—a cold-water jar and a *chaire*, a small ceramic container holding the matcha tea powder wrapped in a *shifuku* silk pouch.

The guests sit down, and the host opens the door and walks in with the tea bowl. The sound created by sliding the ball of the foot forward on the tatami was copied in chanoyu from the Noh theater as "an art of walking." Again, ma, in rhythm and movement, sound and silence. The wastewater receptacle holding the kettle lid rest and a bamboo ladle are brought in, then the door is shut, creating an audible punctuation. The host sits in front of the utensils and after the bamboo ladle is placed on the kettle lid rest with a sharp sound, everyone bows together. The reed blinds outside the tearoom windows are rolled up by the host's assistant. Light now pours through the shoji, changing the mood. The host takes a breath or two and begins the *temae*—the procedure for making tea. *Temae* translates as "point in front." The host's focus is only on what is done here and now while the guests actively observe. Again, the acute viewing angle encourages the focus of energy and attention.

It is said that the best temae is when one is able to practically observe oneself doing the temae as the form becomes part of oneself. In slowly folding a lightly held square of silk cloth the host settles their own breathing and coordinates it with the guests' while developing a certain rhythm. Everyone is quiet. The objects that touch the tea are symbolically purified. The only sound is the kettle's wind in the pines. Thick tea is kneaded with the bamboo whisk and is shared by all the guests from the same bowl. It is passed hand to hand and a bow is offered to "see the bowl off."

Holding a hand-pinched, low-fired black *raku* tea bowl in both hands is like holding the hands of the potter in yours, even though the potter may have lived hundreds of years before you. In the dimness of the teahouse and the darkness of the bowl's glaze, one's sense of touch and smell are accentuated. Placing the bowl on the left palm the small glaze-covered foot allows the curved bottom of the bowl to rest there effortlessly. The right hand steadies the bowl, thumb in front as it is lifted, head bowed, in a gesture of gratitude before partaking of the tea. Next the bowl is turned clockwise to avoid drinking from the front of the bowl designated by the host, purified with a linen cloth and re-turned before being handed to the next guest. The scent of the thick dark green tea, the warmth of the bowl, and at last, the taste of the tea, which is at the center of the chaji, focuses attention on the moment.

After each guest has drunk their tea, the empty bowl is passed back for a closer look. Now the bowl is inspected at leisure since the impetus to pass it along promptly so each guest will have hot tea is gone. The bowl is placed in front on the tatami. Again, the acute-angle observation encourages focused attention. Elbows on knees, the bowl is looked at closely from all sides and turned over so the foot and bottom can also be scrutinized.

At the end of the thick tea procedure, the chaire, tea caddy, *chashaku* tea scoop, and the shifuku pouch are offered for closer viewing by the guests. One by one each guest brings the objects in front of them, places their palms on the tatami and mindfully looks at each object. Then, elbows on knees, the object is picked up and looked at in more detail. When the host comes back, a conversation about the pieces takes place as the host shares their names and provenance. What is the shape and the kiln of the tea caddy? Who made the bamboo tea scoop, and does it have a poetic name? Who made the brocade pouch for the chaire?

The Canadian philosopher Charles Taylor in his book *Cosmic Connections: Poetry in the Age of Disenchantment* (Bellknap, 2024) speaks of the "interspace." Adam Gopnik, in a 2024 essay on Taylor in *The New Yorker* writes: "Art isn't absolute, but it isn't at all arbitrary. Taylor escapes from the divide between subjectivity and objectivity through a concept he calls the 'interspace'—not the inner space where I perceive and enjoy but some resonant atmosphere that exists between me and the world. The sound of the cello in a Schubert trio isn't entirely in the cello, where the sound begins, or entirely between my listening ears, where the experience of structured sound as music happens, but somewhere between the two, where the creation of meaning takes place. The interspace is the phenomenal field of the arts. When we listen to sublime music, then, our experience is not of pleasure but of an overwhelming feeling of encountering and exploring some truth. The music sculpts us, we sculpt the music, and to reduce this to mood misses the cosmic connection that the experience proposes and, quite often, provides." Much of a chaji is experienced in that interspace.

After the thick tea, a basket of charcoal is brought to replenish the fire so the sound of the wind in the pines doesn't die down, and more incense is burnt. The atmosphere in the tearoom becomes more relaxed. The host brings back the ceramic water jar. The guests are offered dried sweets this time and a different whisked tea, not kneaded, is offered. After the guests have had a closer look at the tea container (and how the host has filled and used the powder) and the tea scoop, the host speaks about the utensils.

Talking during chaji can be considered functional talking but this function has both aesthetic and spiritual aspects. It is "scripted" and focused on what is happening right then and there, but certain parts of chaji are held in complete silence. Perhaps rather than functional, conversation during chaji can be considered "mindful talking." Mindful speech rather than mindless talking, if you will. All the elements are closely viewed and then talked about later. This "delayed" talking allows participants to "view" objects with their whole self and not be distracted by words. A pause in the current of narrative is specially created in the chaji script for this purpose.

The host enters again to thank each guest and to say goodbye. The guests thank the host one by one and entreat them not to see them off. The guests look at the flowers and the brazier once again.

The "wind in the pines" is still going strong and the feeling is a little sad since everyone would like to make this moment last. Leaving the teahouse the guests stand outside, knowing that even though they asked the host not to see them off, the door to the tearoom will open and the host and guests will bow together in silence. The host watches until they are out of sight.

Returning to the waiting room through the roji, freshly sprinkled with water, everything in the garden looks brighter and more vivid though the moon is almost up. Time and place are fused and are inseparable. Ma is an experience that unifies both time and place. The Japanese architect Arata Isozaki says: "Space could not be perceived independently of the elements of time, and time was not abstracted as a regulated, homogenous flow, but rather was believed to exist only in relation to movements or space . . . Thus, space was perceived as identical with the events or phenomena occurring in it; that is, space was recognized only in its relation to time . . ." (Isozaki, *Ma: Space–Time in Japan*, Cooper-Hewitt Museum, 1974.)

The guests leave the waiting room following the stepping stones back to the gate, through which they may catch a glimpse of moonlight. (The older version of the character for ma was the character for moon inside the character for gate, 閒, instead of the current form depicting sun inside the gate, 間.)

The host stays alone in the tearoom quietly contemplating, in the accumulated energy of the space. Both host and guests feel transformed by the experience which reverberates long after they exit through the gate. They depart leaving their hearts behind.

Rikyu's grandson Sen Sotan said:

"If asked the nature of chanoyu,
Say it's the sound of windblown pines
In a painting."

Photograph by John Einarsen

ear-opening revelations

moments of ma in music

by Joshua Pearl

Something is waiting for you in the music. It is invisible and inaudible, yet you will know it when you experience it. It is fleeting, but always available. It is ineffable, but accessible. All that is required is attention and patience. It is the gift of *ma* in music.

> *An Invitation: Close your eyes and open your ears. Listen carefully to this moment. What do you hear? Without judgment or analysis, give yourself over to the subjective experience of each new sound as it impresses itself upon your awareness. Take note of what you hear: how some of the sounds around you enter and then exit audibility, while others remain ambient in the background. Perhaps there are some internal sounds in your auditory mix—a static, hum, or ringing resounding from within. Allow your attention to follow that sound just like any other. Be with each sound for as long you can or for as long as it will let you.*

KYOTO, JAPAN. EARLY FALL 1989.

A recently transplanted, twenty-three-year old American classically trained pianist living in Japan, is having his weekly lesson with his sensei—a renowned third generation koto master, in her small house nestled in a bamboo grove in the northwest corner of Kyoto. The student removes his shoes and greets his sensei's mother, then student and sensei share a pot of *sencha* tea and a sweet bean pastry. Afterward, they step into the teaching studio, where the sensei reminds her student how to properly apply the finger picks, and how to set up and tune the koto. She informs him that he will need to endure long periods of kneeling in *seiza* position today.

SENSEI: Shall we start?

STUDENT: Yes, I'm ready.

SENSEI: Today you will practice sounding one single note and that will be all. From that one note you will learn a lot. But not yet. First please listen to me play . . .

She plays a standard piece, but her interpretation is radical. She takes an unusually long time between phrases, several times making the student wonder if the piece is over. Whenever the sensei reenters with a new phrase, she delivers it fiercely, like a cat pouncing on her prey after sitting still and waiting for the right moment. When the piece ends, the sensei moves away from the koto and sits on a nearby floor cushion.

SENSEI: What did you notice?

STUDENT: I noticed you waited a very long time between playing one phrase and another. Why did you do that? How did you know when to come back in?

SENSEI: It is a quality called *ma*. It may be the most important principle found in traditional Japanese music.

STUDENT: What is ma?

SENSEI: Ma is a pregnant pause. It is silent but full of possibility. Ma is a way of playing and a way of listening. The practice of ma involves listening very carefully to the music as it changes, bringing your curiosity, and releasing your expectations. Listening this way allows you to hear with fresh, open ears while also preparing you to respond to what you have heard the instant you can wait no longer—and not a moment sooner. The result is a surprising beauty that mysteriously grows out of the music. Playing and listening this way frees you from metronomic time. It makes the sounds float, as if there were a silent presence supporting each sound you make. First you learn to play this way at slow tempos, later you will be able to do it at fast tempos as well.

STUDENT: I would love to be able to do that!

SENSEI: You will . . . but keep in mind, that ma is not a regular music skill, but a reflex: a way of listening and responding to what you hear. It is cultivated, not mastered. Now please sit next to your koto and prepare to play.

STUDENT: Sitting in seiza hurts my knees!

SENSEI: You can slide your ankles out to one side if you need to, it's okay. Now place your thumb pick on the string closest to you, and let your other fingers drape down naturally on the other strings. When you are ready, lift your hand above the strings and then let your hand fall down very heavily on the top string, catching it diagonally with the corner of the pick. The sound goal will be to make the string ring out for as long as possible. Once you have released the sound from the instrument, immediately shift your attention to listening—to see how long the pitch sustains. Follow the sound as it decays with your full attention until you can no longer hear the pitch. This is the beginning of playing with ma. Being an accomplished musician is always part listening and part playing. As you give your attention to the music, you also want to receive back from the music, as deeply as possible.

Over the five years that follow, the koto sensei teaches the student to think about and experience music in new ways. Rather than hearing discreet, stable sounds, she invites him to hear the quality of the changes as the sounds emerge and disappear.

She encourages him to imagine each sound as being *released* from the body of the instrument rather than the sound being produced by the player. This particular image especially transforms the student's relationship to the instrument. Instead of a koto player, he is now a liberator of sound. He learns that to give his full attention to a sound is, in a sense, to liberate it from obscurity.

These shifts of perspective open the student's ears to the many nuances involved in playing with and experiencing ma in music. The student learns that music has subtle dimensions only revealed when one's ears are attuned to hearing them. In the same way that autostereograms (3D eye puzzles) invite one to relax one's eyes and allow a hidden image to arise spontaneously in the visual field, creating the sudden experience of a new depth perception, ma invites a non-normative way of hearing in which ordinary sounds, existing in linear succession, take on a previously unperceived dimension, full of new information and ripe with delicious acoustic phenomena such as transients, overtones and complex phase patterns, born of the sonic interactions between competing vibrations.

As we learn to listen more closely, we begin to hear many new things in the sounds. Our imagination is active, and our curiosity is piqued. In the process of deepening our listening, ma also extends to us extraordinary moments in which we transcend linear time altogether. By completely focusing our attention on the immediacy of the current sound environment, we tend to lose our sense of other times and other sounds.

> *Now, once again listen carefully to your immediate environment, but this time, try to listen for the moments between the sounds. Listen for the myriad changes that occur as a given sound fades out. Try to stay with the dying sounds as long as you can. Now, as*

before, let it all go and reflect on what you just heard. You may notice that sounds appear and disappear with varying frequency much like the way ocean waves approach and recede from the shore, overlapping with each other, creating rhythmic patterns that are steady but not metronomic. Like listening to the rhythms of the ocean, listening with the spaciousness of ma has the potential to still the mind and relax the body.

■ ■ ■ INTERLUDE ■ ■ ■

JOHN CAGE AND HIS SEARCH FOR SILENCE

John Cage (1912–1992), is considered the father of twentieth century experimental music. His art was born of contradiction. As a gifted student, building upon the legacy of modern Western art music, he studied composition with Austrian serial composer Arnold Schoenberg. But he was also a free spirit, and his spiritual inclinations led him to study with Zen advocate and teacher D.T. Suzuki. As Cage matured, he rejected Schoenberg's attempts to "control sound" through stringent systems and rules, and chose to employ the Zen principles of emptiness and beginner's mind by using music composition as a device for exploring what happens when we let go of our illusions of control and let sounds simply exist as they are.

In 1952, he attempted to introduce his radical ideas to classical music audiences. With his now famous composition entitled *Silence* (or *4'33"*) he invited the audience to listen mindfully for the inherent musicality of each and every sound that could be heard in the performance venue—not just "musical" sounds but also the rustling of programs, the awkwardly echoing cough that shatters the formality of the concert hall, and the sounds from outside that manage to penetrate the hall. By instructing the performer to provide a gesture such as opening or shutting the lid of the piano in order to signify a new section, Cage presented audiences with three intervals of time (movements) to sonically contemplate what they were hearing. The original performance lasted approximately 4 minutes and 33 seconds—the reason for the alternate title.

Before Cage composed this piece, he went on a personal search for the experience of absolute silence by stepping into a 100 percent hermetically sealed soundproof anechoic chamber. After a brief time, he came out and complained to the staff that there was something wrong with the chamber: there were two sounds getting in—one low pitched and one high pitched. The explanation he received was that the room was, in fact, silent, and all the sounds he heard were emanating from his own body's nervous, respiratory and circulatory systems. This explanation convinced him there was no such thing as actual silence, that silence was an abstraction—nothing we could actually ever hear, but, nonetheless an essential sonic *presence* that underlies all sounds, allowing them to be heard.

KYOTO, JAPAN. LATE FALL 1989.

In November 1989, John Cage, then seventy-seven years old, was in Japan to receive the prestigious Kyoto Prize honoring his lifetime of bold experimentation. A journalist friend of the aforementioned student knew of the student's interest in Cage's research on the topic of silence, and set up a meeting. The next day, the student met with John Cage for an hour in his hotel room.

Seated on a green sofa behind a glass coffee table, Cage offered the student a seat on an adjacent chair and began to describe his philosophy of sound. He said that if we listen single-mindedly, we will hear that each unique sound emanates from a specific center point. He explained that the chance procedures he used in his compositions were designed to free the sounds from the tyranny of the composer's will.

John Cage not only explained his philosophy of sound, he embodied it. In Cage's presence, the student could not help but listen more closely to all the sounds around him, as if the deep attention Cage paid to all the sounds in the room amplified them for others in the vicinity. This opened the student's ears to a world of new sounds in the room, those coming in from the hallway, those produced by the heating and ventilation system, and those penetrating the muffling filter of closed hotel room windows. All the sounds took on more life and resonance, and silence was the source they all shared. Cage did not speak directly about ma, but his mode of listening helped the student deepen the lessons he had been receiving from his koto sensei, and he began to apply them to all aspects of his music making.

Like John Cage's compositions, ma is an open invitation to listen for silence rather than for sound. But in reality, silence and sound are not binary—there is a wide spectrum of dynamics ranging from the completely inaudible to physically painful. To further complicate the matter, each point on the sound–silence spectrum also breaks down into infinitely finer increments of dynamic nuance waiting to be discovered, each point opening up a universe of distinct tonal and timbral qualities. Ma perpetually invites us to explore the entire dynamic spectrum and to cultivate the ability to discern these finer increments of musical experience.

> *What is it that exists between sounds? What is it that exists around each separate sound? Once again, open your ears and close your eyes. As you expand your hearing, listen for the silences between and around the sounds and witness how they "hold" the sounds, binding them to each other while also creating a cushion for containing each specific sound. As John Cage revealed, silence is not empty. It is full of an incredible energy and exists as a wellspring of potential from which all sounds emerge. Silence is what makes music possible. Silence is what makes ma in music perceptible.*

KYOTO, JAPAN. WINTER 1990.

Not long after his fortuitous meeting with John Cage, the student was presented with another rare opportunity, again thanks to his journalist friend. This time, he was invited to play piano, collaborating, rehearsing and performing in a concert of mostly improvised music, together with an ensemble of diverse musicians, including the renowned Sudanese *oud* lute virtuoso, Hamza el Din, and the legendary Indian *bansuri* flute master, Pandit Hariprasad Chaurasia. The concert was part of a conference honoring the work of author and physicist Fritjof Capra and promoting awareness of environmental and humanitarian crises plaguing the planet. The concert was intended to give conference attendees a visceral experience of healing and presence through music, a chance to let go of their rational minds and settle into a deeper state of being. After a week of meetings and rehearsals, the musicians were ready to perform.

At the beginning of the concert, as the lights slowly faded out, the ambient drone of the tambura slowly faded in. After a few minutes of simply sitting on stage and listening with everybody else, Hariprasad Chaurasia picked up his flute and put it to his lips, but he did not yet make a sound. A palpable curiosity and tension filled the auditorium. After what seemed like almost too long a pause, he finally exhaled into his instrument, emoting a single sustaining pitch. As the flute sounded, the tension in the auditorium, born of a collective anticipation and impatience, instantly dissipated and in its place was a deepening of collective attention. A sense of ma filled the space.

Chaurasia sustained that single pitch for a long time, until he gradually—almost imperceptibly—slid the pitch downward by the musical interval of a half step, patiently sliding until the flute fully arrived at a distinct second pitch, at which time he settled into the new arrival point and let out the rest of his breath. The student didn't know exactly how long that extraordinary musical event lasted, but the moment felt eternal.

Though the concert had barely begun, the student's sense of time was inexplicably altered, the audience was transfixed, and even the visual appearance of the room seemed strangely transformed. The student surmised that Chaurasia literally took his time before playing, then took creative ownership of that time once he started

As the flute sounded, the tension in the auditorium, born of a collective anticipation and impatience, instantly dissipated and in its place was a deepening of collective attention. A sense of ma filled the space.

Photograph by John Einarsen

playing, implicitly giving the audience permission to do the same.

The rest of the concert provided a series of musical treasures for the student to ponder, and the thrill of playing with these master musicians at such a young age reinforced the student's desire to inhabit the spaces between sounds much more deeply. The student never forgot those first moments of the concert, when he fully experienced the profound transformative potential of ma in music for the first time. The immediacy of the initial bansuri pitch and Chaurasia's patient descent between two simple pitches would override every other detail about that concert in the student's memory.

In the thirty years since these formative, ear-opening moments, the student continued to listen for the empty spaces between sounds and inhabit the pregnant pauses between phrases. He discovered that many musicians intuitively understand how to play with ma even if they have never been exposed to the concept. After decades of contemplating and cultivating ma, the student trained to become a clinical music therapist and to this day uses ma to hold the space for his patients to express themselves. The student has not mastered ma but has experienced it enough to write about it. His appreciation for and love of ma inspired him to write this essay.

> *Every moment offers the opportunity to practice ma, to listen with new ears. Many of those moments will go by unrequited, but ma does not hold grudges. No matter how often you may forget to listen with ma, there is still (and always) the possibility of trying again, and in doing so, what was previously inaudible is revealed.*

"Ma is a way of playing and a way of listening."

Beauty Playing the Koto Zither
by Suzuki Harunobu
Tokyo National Museum
See "ear-opening revelations," page 71.

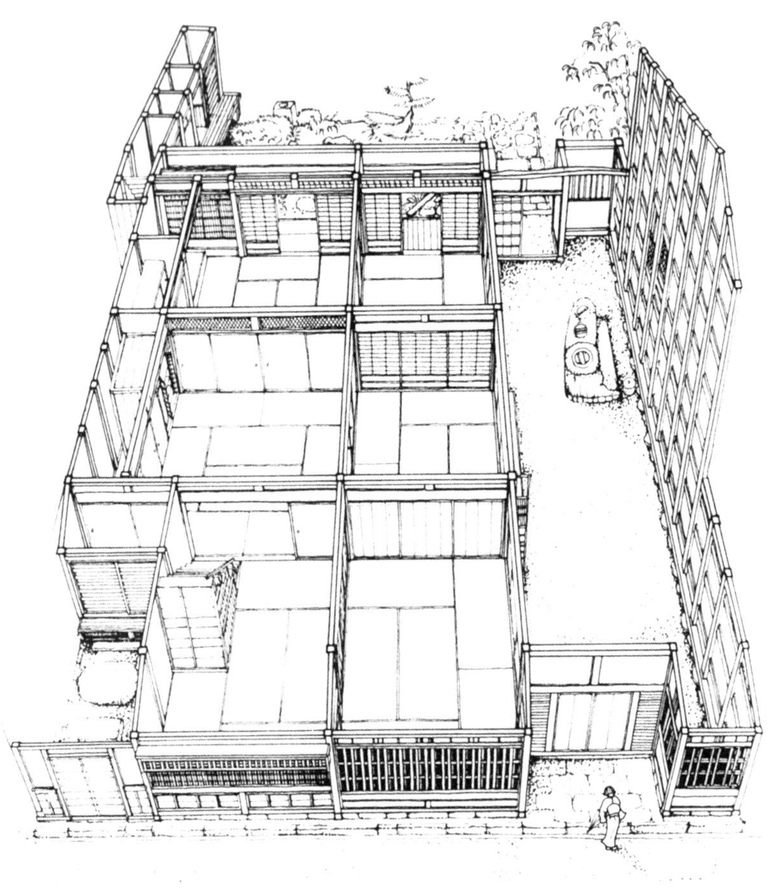

Isometric sketch of a typical machiya townhouse of Nara Prefecture in Imaecho, showing a doma as a kitchen and workspace
(From *Nihon no Minka*, Gakken, Tokyo 1980).
See "ma—place, space, void," page 11.

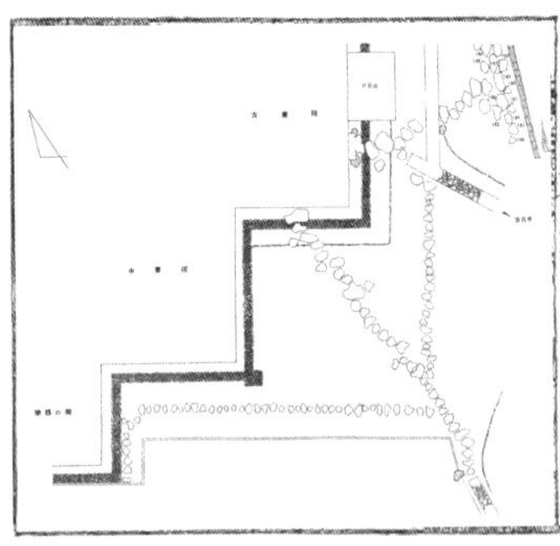

LEFT: *Tobi-ishi* stepping stones, spaced to manipulate the walker's speed and direction. (From Niwa Tyazawa, *The Stepping Stones in Katsura Detached Palace*, Shokokusha, Tokyo, 1955); BELOW: Showing approaches to a house. (Reproduced from Chikusan Teizoden, a Japanese work). From *Japanese Homes and their Surroundings* by Edward S. Morse. Harper & Bros. 1885.
See "ma—place, space, void," page 11.

A garden view at Fukuchi-in Temple at Koyasan, Wakayama Prefecture. Photograph by Stephen Mansfield. See "some gravel, some stones," page 33.

Path at Okochi Sanso Villa, Kyoto. Photograph by Allan Mandell.
See "invitations to stillness," page 45.

"Japanese gardens . . . are perfectly suited as spaces for withdrawal, repose and as places where one seeks order in a disorderly world."

A garden view at Koto-in, a sub-temple of Daitokuji Temple, Kyoto. Photograph by Allan Mandell. See "invitations to stillness," page 45.

The Cathedral by Miya Ando. See "between form and emptiness," page 89.

Miya Ando.

Obon by Miya Ando, photographed by Lee Ufan. See "between form and emptiness," page 89.

生 / *Life*, 2019. Mixed media, each piece 9 x 6.5 in (23 x 17 cm)

All of the characters on each piece are the same, "life." In 2009, I began to write the character "life" continuously on small pieces of paper to pray for children who had died due to hunger-related causes. One day, when I gazed at many of the "life" pieces on a wall in my studio, each of the characters looked like the faces and figures of people. At that moment, I realized that I could express

diversity through my works. All of the characters are the same, “life,” but each one is expressed differently on various kinds of paper from around the world. If there are a hundred people, there are a hundred ways of life.
See “animating ma,” by Nakajima Hiroyuki, page 97.

“Can something appear out of nothing?
Can truth strike you like a lightning bolt in blue skies?
Do mountains smile when all beings open their eyes?”

This page and facing page: From the series *Tamashi* by Morgan Fisher.
See "the heart of the matter," page 113.

This page and facing page: photographs by Magdalena Rittenhouse. See "moments of silence and stillness," page 123.

"Gates, thresholds, screens and passages—intermediary zones created to gently separate the inside from the outside, the sacred from the profane, the safe and tamed from the unfamiliar."

“Isolation, metaphysically at least, is a landscape we know, explore, and at times get lost in.”

Photographs by Kit Pancoast Nagamura. See "on isolation," page 127.

Kit Pancoast Nagamura. See "on isolation," page 127.

Kit Pancoast Nagamura. See "on isolation," page 127.

"*Ma-ai* is the heartbeat of any encounter in martial arts, blending precision, timing, and psychological insight."

Alexander Bennett and "the deadly dance of distance," see page 133.

Image by Atticus Sims.
See "constructing reality," page 139.

“This is the Buddhist notion of emptiness. Emptiness doesn’t mean that this is an empty void. People use that word, but it’s not void. It’s the connections, relationships, interactions—that is what is meant by emptiness.”

Image by Atticus Sims.
See “constructing reality,” page 139.

“According to certain Buddhist traditions, if you train more you can see things more as they are in actuality, but, at the same time, there is a limit to our nature as human beings.”

Images by Atticus Sims.
See "constructing reality," page 139.

"photographic ma" by Robert van Koesveld, see page 149.

"the contemplative gaze," by Edward A. Burger, see page 81.

"... within us is this great mindscape, and what goes on in there defines what goes on out here, in life and how we experience the world."

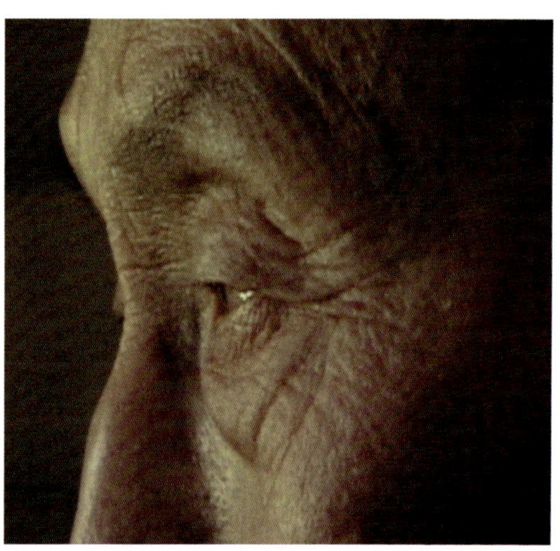

"the contemplative gaze," by Edward A. Burger, see facing page.

"What matters is the gaze. With the gaze, you are on the Path."

the contemplative gaze

living with an awareness of mind

by Edward A. Burger

It was right around the time I was heading into college that I started getting interested in the contemplative life. I was reading a lot, and Hesse, Salinger, Maugham and Kerouac were taking me on epic, soulful adventures. Their writing had an incandescence—lit from the inside with inquiry and a spiritual longing.

Looking back, what I found in their writing was a shift in perspective toward a wider view of life. One that respects the entire spectrum of human experience—from joy to pain and everything in between. There is a dark aspect to this world, and we are most often encouraged to turn away from that shadow. I was frustrated by these messages around me—from billboards, television and checkout-counter magazines—that said happiness is out there somewhere, in the opposite direction of the darkness. That you find happiness with your back toward sorrow, pain, longing and disappointment. There was a whole part of life that felt hidden but full of meaning; taboo but honest. I did not want to abandon that darkness, as though it did not matter, and in me began to boil an eagerness to rebel against that great perpetuating myth about happiness.

When I was a student at the College of Wooster, by a miracle of serendipity and some great advice from my academic advisor, I landed in Dr. Ishwar Harris's course on Buddhism. When I heard the Buddha's life story for the first time, it was revelatory. I do not think I was really conscious of it at the time, but the Buddha embodied this very sense of rebellion to me. I learned that the Buddha was a prince whose parents cloistered him in a palace, hiding him from the inevitabilities of sickness, old age and death. But he abandoned palace life and struck out in the night, cutting off his royal locks, the symbol of his princely rank, to enter into the forest to meditate and live the contemplative life. He turned his gaze inward and committed his entire being to inner cultivation. He left us the Dharma—practical and simple, yet evolutive teachings on how to be a kinder, wiser being in this world. I had found my shift in perspective, and with it, a lifetime of creative exploration.

> *Subhuti, if a bodhisattva should thus claim,*
> *"I shall bring about the transformation of a world,"*
> *such a claim would be untrue. And how so?*
> *The transformation of a world, Subhuti,*
> *the "transformation of a world" is said by the*
> *Tathagata to be no transformation. Thus is it called*
> *the "transformation of a world."*
>
> —*The Diamond Sutra*, trans Red Pine

By the end of my first year at the college, my exploration of Buddhist thought and culture was deepening as was my interest in art. I started reading the poems of the T'ang Dynasty hermit Cold Mountain. Jack Kerouac affectionately called him a "Zen Lunatic" and seemed to identify with his aesthetic sensibility and his rebellious tone, and so did I. Around that time, Bill Porter wrote the book *Road to Heaven*. In it, we learn there are hermits like Cold Mountain living in China now, just like the old days. So, after school, off I went to find Cold Mountain myself.

In my film, *The Mountain Path* (2020), you meet the hermit monk whom I still call my teacher today. Shifu taught me how to read scripture, and he taught me how to meditate. He is a true mountain monk, with a direct and creative sensibility. He taught me how to sit and explore the forms and capacities of my mind in a way that spoke straight to me. Every time I hiked down that mountain trail, the world seemed a little different than it did on the way up. And over the many years of meditation practice to follow, in both Chan[1] and Vipassana traditions, a whole new way of seeing and engaging the world started to emerge within me—a way of seeing I call the "contemplative gaze."

Contemplative gaze means living with an awareness of mind—just the basic recognition that within us is this great mindscape, and what goes on in there defines what goes on out here, in life and how we experience the world.

First, we turn our gaze inward and discover our capacity to pay attention and observe our own body and mind. We work on increasing the fidelity of that attention, the breadth and depth of observation. At first, every thread of our being rebels. It feels awkward and unnatural, even painful. But we learn to stay put, sit still, and stick with it. Slowly, as if a light were turned on, shapes begin to emerge. The forms and structures of the mind and of the self-mechanism gain definition as they emerge from the shadows. Mind becomes something workable, something we can relate to. And we can explore in that space. Over time the contemplative gaze inward becomes so strong and resolute that even as we look outward, we hold that gaze, unwaveringly, and carry it out into the world and into our lives. This is a miraculous thing, a blossoming of the contemplative gaze. The inner realm and the outer realm unite into a single, unified field of experience.

The contemplative gaze is not necessarily an enlightened gaze—it is just a shift in perspective that happens naturally when we practice meditation. We may discover ourselves standing anywhere

1. I use "Zen" when referring to this tradition of approaching and cultivating the Buddhadharma in general, "Chan" when I am talking about Zen Buddhism in China.

on the spectrum from confused to enlightened, and that does not matter here. What matters is the gaze. With the gaze, you are on the Path. And the Path is what Buddhist contemplatives share regardless of where we find ourselves on it.

Regardless of the tradition practiced, or by what method you cultivate it, for me, this contemplative gaze is a fundamental shift toward an artistic perspective—from a life lived for what we see, to a life lived for *how* we see. It is a shift from distraction toward presence. From a reactive relationship with the world toward an illuminating gaze upon the world. This is a definitive contemplative Buddhist experience. We are not talking about states of euphoria or being carried off somewhere. Inherent in this gaze itself is a power to heal and evolve—to move toward Buddhahood.

New art for an old path

Traditional Buddhist art forms like calligraphy, landscape painting, poetry and narrative have given shape to the contemplative experience for many centuries. Years ago, I had a book on the Zen arts that I cherished. In it was a big, beautiful black-and-white photo of the Ryoanji rock garden in Kyoto. A couple of years ago, my wife and I visited that garden. The first glance through the frame of dark timber pillars and roof beams took my breath away. From the viewing veranda, the precision of the craftsmanship of the whole garden, the angles, the composition, the textures—is like being in the presence of mind itself. There is a skillful unity of form and meaning that resonates with the mindscape within us, lights it up, and grounds us in presence and attention. I thought, there has got to be a way to make cinema like this.

The distinctive multidimensional quality of the cinema-viewing experience makes it suitable for celebrating, sharing and exploring the Buddhist contemplative experience as I know it and as I see others living it. I look for inspiration from cinema masters like Tarkovsky, Ozu, Herzog, Varda, Malick and Lynch, who each in their own way wrestle with the formal qualities of cinema itself

because they know that's where it happens—bringing to life the inner world of their characters. They work at such a transcendent depth in their art, working with cinema as a language to express a mysterious and profound inquiry into human experience, that I think their cinema embodies something universally contemplative. In their work, I recognize the contemplative principles that I want to explore though film as a Buddhist artist.

The inner landscapes

If a film succeeds in making the audience comfortable with the shifting between inner and outer realms of vision, then the contemplative gaze finds its full fruition when we can no longer say for certain if what we are seeing on the cinema screen is the character's gaze upon their world, or upon themselves—their inward gaze. Now we are working with both what the character sees and how the character sees, simultaneously. We are in the contemplative gaze.

We look out at mountain landscapes, or a great sprawl of farmland or a bamboo forest, and these landscapes are nothing other than the character's own inner landscapes. Now the film can play in that space, with all elements of landscape available—like a drop of rain or a drifting cloud, an insect or an ox, swift and fleeting birds.

Years ago, at a monastery in the north of China, a close teacher of mine[2] said to me: "A buddha is a being, like you or I, who has awoken from the dream of ignorance. That makes us all dreaming buddhas." Many cinema artists have wrestled with the experience of dreams in cinema. But how to tackle *the* dream? Approaching cinema with the same techniques as the great cinema masters, we can carry the audience along on a trip into the inner landscapes. And that is really great cinema, but it is not Buddhist contemplative cinema. What makes *Buddhist* contemplative cinema is the vision, the gaze, that recognizes the inner landscape, the emptiness of the *big* dream, and the aspiration to wake up.

2. Ven. Ming Ying, who at that time was the senior prior at Bailin Chan Monastery.

Obon. Photograph by Lee Ufan.

between form and emptiness

Leanne Ogasawara interviews artist Miya Ando

A descendant on her mother's side of Bizen sword-makers and Buddhist priests, American artist Miya Ando's childhood was spent between her family's temple in Okayama, Japan and the Californian redwood forests near Santa Cruz. Her works in metal, canvas and sculpture are deeply rooted in Buddhist philosophy and are meditations on the human experience of time, the seasons, and ephemerality. In addition to her numerous solo exhibitions, one of her large-scale works was exhibited at the 56th Venice Biennale in 2015, in the historic Museo di Palazzo Grimani. This interview took place by email during the Covid pandemic.

OGASAWARA: *Miya, thank you for talking with us during these strange times of Covid-19. I think the lockdown might be easier for introverts. Are you finding this to be a fruitful time for making art?*

ANDO: I'm very happy being alone all day in my studio not speaking to anyone, so that part of the lockdown is something that I don't mind at all. I'm finding this period to be reflective and

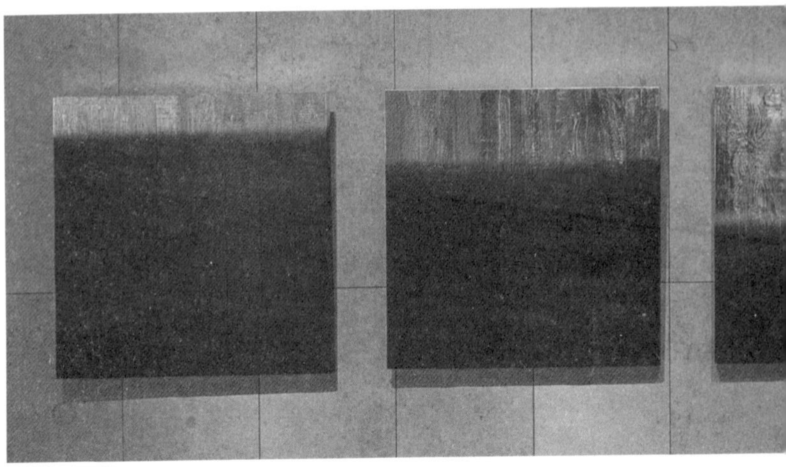

Tides (Shou Sugi Ban)

fruitful; I enjoy the quietude. I'm also very concerned about the deaths and danger.

You spent your childhood in the forests of Santa Cruz, as well as in a Buddhist temple in Japan. I wonder if you could discuss two specific works that relate to these different places?

I made *The Cathedral* (*The Shrine of Trees, The Sisters and the Mother*) for an exhibition at the Museum of Art and History in Lancaster, California in 2018. It is a homage to the Santa Cruz mountains where I grew up. I lived on twenty-five acres of redwood forest, very rural and off the grid. My father once made my sister and I a tree house in a cathedral of redwood trees.

What is a cathedral of redwood trees? I've never heard that expression.

A naturally occurring ring of trees is called a "cathedral." In the center is the oldest, largest tree. It drops seeds, which become seedlings and eventually large trees surround the center tree. There is a natural ring of redwood trees (more than 200 feet [60 m] tall) where I lived in the Santa Cruz mountains. In the center of the

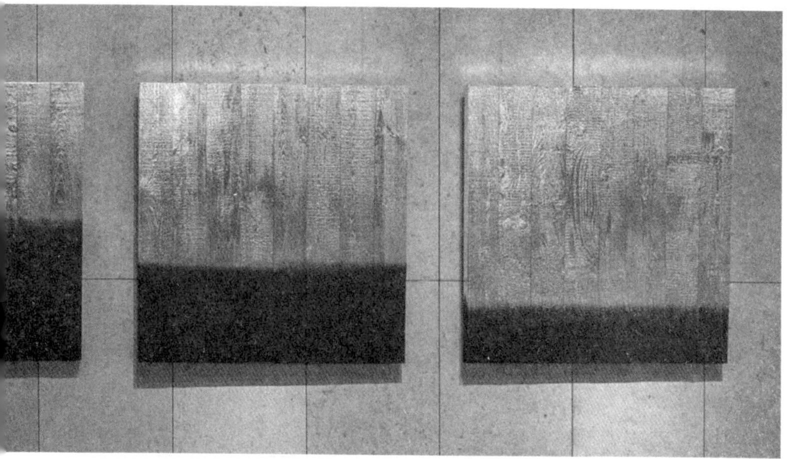

ring was a "mother" tree that had been struck by lightning and was charred black. I have been fascinated by the fact that within a ring of trees, if the "mother" tree suffers serious damage the trees around it send glucose via their roots to the dying tree and keep it alive, sometimes for decades. The piece invites visitors to enter the ring of trees, created with gossamer silk chiffon panels, aiming to create a tranquil and contemplative immersive environment.

California's redwood trees are a sight to behold . . .

Yes. They are the largest living organisms on earth and some of the oldest. I've seen these giants sway and bow in thundering rain and during extreme storms—and yet they stand. I always thought that these trees are so wise, they've seen it all and they are majestic and elegant. I'd like to be just like them. I've also heard a redwood tree fall in a storm and the crashing sound is like no other.

Where is your family's temple located in Japan? Which sect is it?

My grandfather was the head priest of a Nichiren temple in Okayama. Now my cousin has taken the position.

Is there a particular work that reflects your time there?

I've made several works in homage to the Japanese part of my upbringing. *72 Ko (Seasons)* is a grid of 72 paintings (pigment and urethane) I made in 2018 for an exhibition in Singapore. There are 72 seasons in the ancient Japanese calendar. When I was a child, I'd watch my grandmother put on her kimono and take careful time planning the color of her obi and various parts of the outfit. Every decision was based upon the perfect color of the season. This acute attention and respect for nature made a huge impression on me. It felt so refined to be so aware of this type of harmony with nature.

Could you tell us about your apprenticeship with Hattori Studio and your family's background in metal-working?

My ancestor Ando Yoshiro Masakatsu was a swordsmith. Notably, he created a sword that is considered a national treasure of Japan. I apprenticed at Hattori Studio when I was younger, and learned respect for the materials, techniques and practices of metallurgy.

In November 2019 your solo show Form Is Emptiness, Emptiness is Form opened at the Asia Society in Houston. Could you tell us a little about the show?

The exhibition's title is from the cherished Mahayana text the *Heart Sutra*, and my works evoke the idea of ephemerality through images of water and light, as well as chemical and electrical processes.

We really see your experience studying metallurgy in Tides (Shou Sugi Ban). *On my computer screen it seems painted, or like a photograph. What is so fascinating is that this is actually metal and wood, that has undergone a radical transformation.*

The wood is reclaimed redwood from the Santa Cruz mountains. I charred it in the ancient technique of *shou sugi ban* (or *yakisugi*), which is a material that reminds me of Okayama. The Buddhist temple that I lived in as a child and also all the houses in the area are clad in shou sugi ban. The traditional wood that is used is cedar (*sugi*), but in this case I selected a material that is of my other upbringing in Northern California. I'm intrigued by this material of transformation and the idea that one burns or destroys something in order to protect oneself and one's home. (Shou sugi ban is used as fireproofing and as a bug repellent in Japan). I also like the metaphor of a material undergoing intense duress and coming out stronger in the end. The composition of *Tides* is inspired by tides moving in and out.

For this exhibition I was very interested in investigating the interaction of elements and their transformation as well—as a transformation in the mind. The *karesansui* garden at Ryoanji temple is comprised of rocks, but the imagery conjured is of the sea, the Milky Way, a tiger swimming with cubs across a body of water, all sorts of things. I find this of interest. Could a charred piece of wood evoke the tides, or perhaps, in the example of my sculpture *Mizukagami*, a hammered stainless sheet of metal might evoke a body of water?

Your work Clouds *is also a breathtaking exploration in transformation.*

Like fire, it is another way to explore transformation and change. And though in *Tides*, fire is the agent, the title reflects water. Clouds have fascinated me for a long time, I'm very interested in clouds as a perfect vocabulary for impermanence. Clouds are so evanescent, ever changing and moving. However, clouds are water and the change of state of these elements has interested me.

Could you tell us a little about your work, Ryoanji*?*

I recreated the Ryoanji garden at one-third scale for my exhibition. I am very interested in karesansui rock gardens in general, but in particular I have been mystified and captivated by Ryoanji since I

Above and inset, facing page: *Ryoanji*

was a girl. My investigation begins with the idea of Ryoanji being a *mutei* (garden of emptiness) and looking deeper into the idea of emptiness, within the context of the *Heart Sutra*, was the genesis of this project. Traditionally, one may chant the *Heart Sutra* before viewing gardens in Japan and this has always struck me. My exploration of transformation is executed with materiality, changing elements (rock to a more ephemeral element: wood), charring the wood and in some ways minimizing even further the forms of the rock groupings.

You have mentioned both Buddhism and quantum mechanics in talking about your current work. In quantum mechanics, matter and energy are constantly in flux—continuously transforming. I wonder how you came to focus on notions of time as a way to explore ephemerality?

I've always been interested in the idea of impermanence in Buddhist thought. Living in Okayama with my grandparents influenced me

quite a bit, as impermanence and nature—the recognition of the beauty in all things as transitory—was instilled in me from a young age. Looking deeper at time and temporality led me to physics and I realized the striking similarities that exist in both Buddhism and science. I have been exploring this in my work ever since.

It is so interesting. We know that the chair we are sitting on is composed of a kind of empty space. Harder to conceive of is the way form is generated from a vacuum. Or that everything that exists "is" composed of fields in a vacuum.

The *Heart Sutra*, which informed the exhibition at the Asia Society discusses this notion. "Form is emptiness and emptiness is form" speaks to the idea that all things are ephemeral. The fundamental nature of reality is that all constituent forms that make up the universe are temporary (Buddhism and quantum physics). Since everything is in a constant state of flux, nothing has a fixed identity.

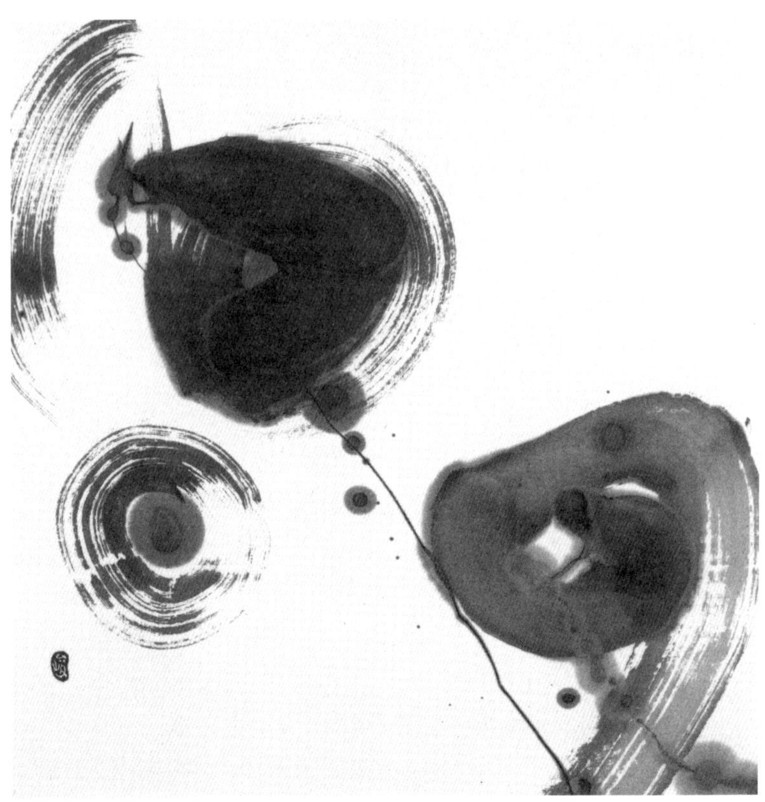

間 / *Interval*, 1999. Chinese ink on paper,
13 x 13 in (34 x 34 cm).

間 / *Interval*

To symbolize Japan's cultural tradition, I thought of the character for "interval" (*ma*). A blank space in a picture, a rest in music and a pause in dance, "interval" is different from "emptiness." It is something which awakens viewers' imagination. In Japanese, this character is used in words for basic matter, for example "human," "time" and "space."

animating ma

the calligraphic art of Nakajima Hiroyuki

by Nakajima Hiroyuki

Born in Japan in 1956, Nakajima Hiroyuki began to learn Japanese calligraphy at six years of age and continued to practice while enrolled in industrial engineering with a focus on architectonics in postgraduate studies at Chiba University. Japanese calligraphy is a highly developed traditional art form, and most professional calligraphers become teachers in private schools, but he sought another way to live, as a master of Japanese calligraphy. In his thirties, Nakajima chose to become an artist, creating works based on Japanese calligraphy. In 2000, he held a private exhibition in a contemporary art gallery in Rome, his first show in Europe. At that time, he began to do calligraphy performances. His movements are influenced by tai chi, which he has been practicing since his twenties. Since 2000, he has continued to hold exhibitions and performances in Italy, France, Finland, Germany and the US. In 2006, he was invited to exhibit and perform at the 60th Avignon Festival, an international stage art festival in France. In 2008, he set up a studio in Milan, Italy. www.nakajimahiroyuki.com

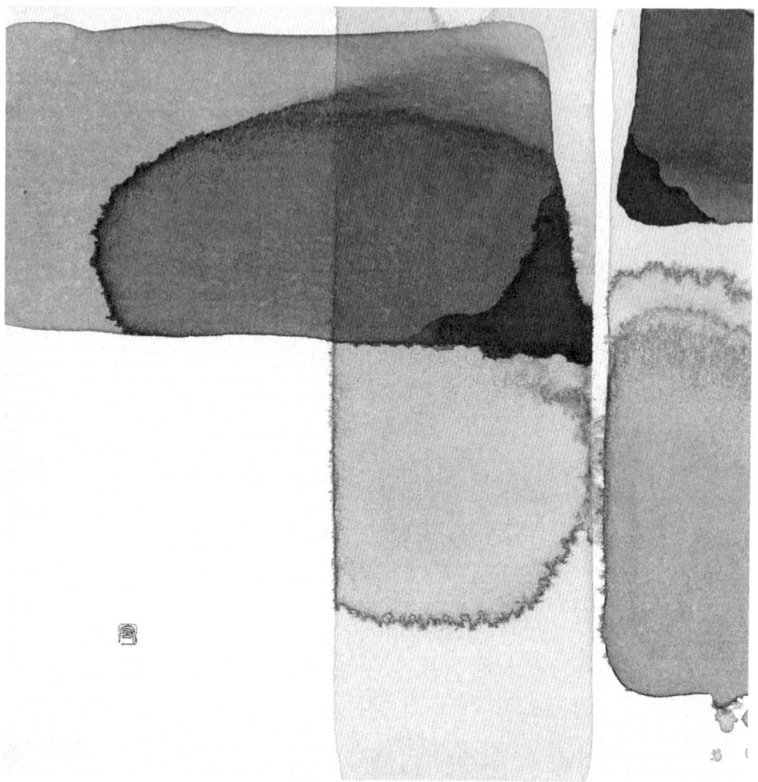

水 / *Water 1*, 2008. Chinese ink on canvas,
12 x 15.5 in (30 x 40 cm).

水 / *Water 1*

I applied Chinese ink gently to the canvas on the floor, and it began to "swim" on the canvas like a living creature. By next morning, the work had completely dried, and the traces where the ink and the canvas had played together during the night were left behind. They are unexpected and beyond the control of my hands. But I try to positively accept this and complete my works together with the power of nature. I think what we have to consider now is not "how we control nature for ourselves," but "how we control ourselves for nature."

水 / *Water 2*, 2011. Chinese ink, dye on paper,
13 x 13 in (34 x 34 cm).

水 / *Water 2*

Rain flows into a river, which pours into the sea, forms clouds and falls again on the earth. Water is always changing, is never satisfied with the present situation. Water always flows into a lower place, remains horizontal and never competes with others. Water is so flexible that it fits into any environment. Water is not only an essential element for our lives, but also offers suggestions for a good way of living.

月 / *Moon*

A new moon, a crescent moon, a half moon, a full moon . . . then a new moon. The moon waxes and wanes periodically. It symbolizes the idea of metempsychosis. Everything on earth changes from moment to moment. All things are in flux through the endless circle of birth, death and rebirth.

月 / *Moon*, 2014. Chinese ink, gold on paper, 27 x 27 in (68 x 68 cm).

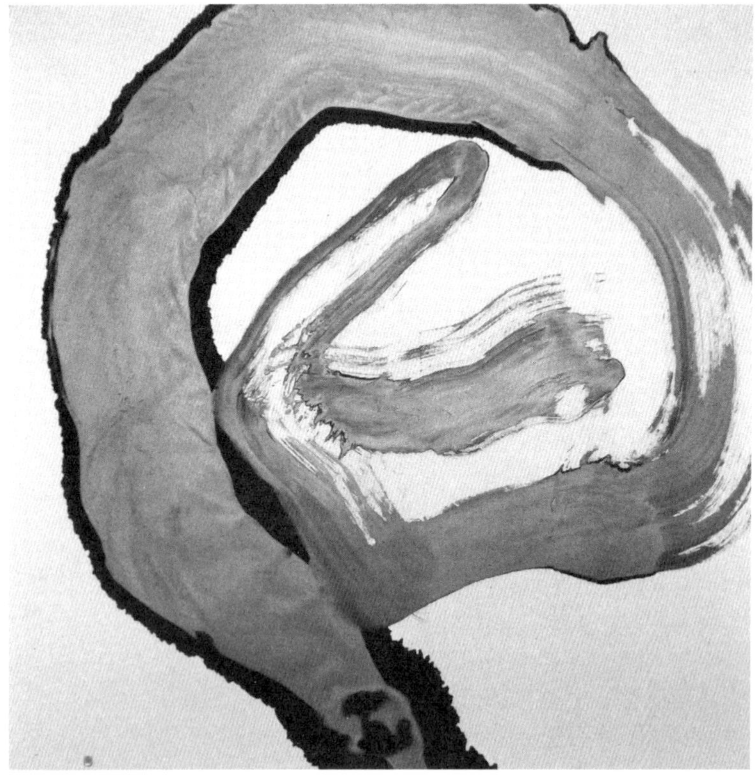

風 / *Wind*, 2011. Chinese ink on paper, 67 x 27 in (171 x 69 cm)

風 / *Wind*

I do not know from where the wind has come. I do not know where the wind will go. Even if I regret the past and worry about the future, I can do nothing about them. I will live in the present, with all my might, feeling the wind of the present moment.

Our Lady of Compassion, displayed in a tokonoma alcove, in a composition that fits the silver ratio.

yohaku and ma in Japanese visual arts

by Hikaru Hirata-Miyakawa

I feel that I exist in a special kind of *ma* called *hazama.* Usually hazama is translated into English as "arrow-slit," but in this case, I mean the narrow interstice between Asian and Western cultures.

Even though my artistic style has been surrealistic/visionary and I have been researching Leonardo da Vinci for over fifty years—together with being a performer of European classical music, vocally and instrumentally—I am proud of my Japanese heritage since I'm distantly connected to the Taisho Emperor (1879–1926). My great-grandfather Yasujiro Kobayashi Jr and the Taisho Emperor were foster brothers, as the Meiji Emperor ordered my great-great-grandmother to be the future Taisho Emperor's wet-nurse. This came about partially because my great-great-grandfather Yasujiro Kobayashi Sr was a purveyor and official artisan to the imperial household, and official imperial educator to the crown prince. He served two Japanese emperors, Meiji and Taisho, who were at the time considered to be divinities. Yasujiro Jr was also an official imperial artisan to the Showa Emperor.

The house I partially grew up in had an adjunct workshop which welcomed visitors; its gift shop storefront had been established at the time of the fourth Tokugawa shogun, Ietsuna, who ruled from 1651 to 1680. The unique *shoin-zukuri* style interior of the main house had been remodeled by Yasujiro Jr.

As a first-born great-grandson, I was given a special education and was even treated as the reincarnation of Yasujiro Jr. My lessons as a child were focused on art, music and writing. I ate, breathed and lived the traditional cultures of the highest grade unconsciously, and my subsequent studies and interest in the West were built upon this very traditional Japanese spirit. As a curious-minded boy, I often visited and studied the tools in the workshop of my deceased great-grandfather, feeling the presence of the spirits of my ancestors. In addition, thanks to my late father, a math and science wizard who excelled in computational math, geometry, and communication skills, I was educated about ratios and proportions and other important aspects of artistic composition.

My purpose, however, became not to revive Japanese artisan tradition, but rather to work within the overlap between two cultures—East and West. Due to my unique experiences in Japan and abroad, I can see some things that are not commonly perceived.

At the time of writing I have been reworking a painting shown previously at The Terminal gallery in Kyoto, a *machiya* traditional town-house with a shoin-zukuri interior featuring a *tokonoma* altar-like space originally intended for personal worship within Buddhism. While Japanese traditional painted images (including calligraphy) on hanging scrolls may often be asymmetrical, the way the scroll is hung, in the center of the tokonoma wall, is symmetrical (see page 102).

It may be that symmetry brings out a sense of peace. The wall space surrounding the hanging scroll can be recognized as *yohaku*, meaning "blank space," complementing the main image. Thus the tokonoma should not be isolated and considered alone, independently. The space next to it, called *tokowaki,* must also be considered since the two viewed together create a sense of balance and harmony. The surrounding empty space becomes ma or yohaku.

Whether described as yohaku or *liubai* in Chinese, reflecting the philosophy of Laozi, Confucius and of Buddhism, what appears as empty space is deliberate—an "intended blank." This space in calligraphy is unique since it is abstract, unlike in *sansui* ink landscape paintings where viewers can imagine some fantastic scenery behind this blank space. Whether in calligraphy or paintings, this seemingly empty space creates a strong impression of balance and harmony. It has a highly potent energy of its own. At the same time, it allows viewers to breathe, mentally and psychologically.

If you compare Western to Eastern art it is apparent that Western paintings tend to be busy, with the entire canvas filled, since blank space is considered unfinished. There is almost no space for the viewers' imagination and participation. The theme and its representation is imposed upon the viewers.

Psychologically, yohaku can be related to or equated to *yoyu*, a kind of spatial margin. Yoyu in space allows you to move relatively freely. It is not a tight fit nor is it stifling. It gives you a sense of natural flow. You are mentally and psychologically free to move, and it invites you in.

Balance and counterbalance are also essential elements of ma, particularly when curating an exhibition space. Yohaku can counterbalance the main subject of a display with certain intensity created by themes, tones, colors, gradations or sizes. Basically, the walls become the yohaku, so ma needs to be considered.

The silver ratio

Conformity to proportional conventions is also an important element in Japanese visual arts, including *byobu* folding screens, *fusuma* sliding screens and even *sensu* folding fans. I have been examining works by the Rinpa-style painters Tawaraya Sotatsu (1570–1643) and Ogata Korin (1658–1716) from the point of view of the silver ratio. There are two types of silver ratio; one of them is quite familiar since it is applied to the proportions of paper

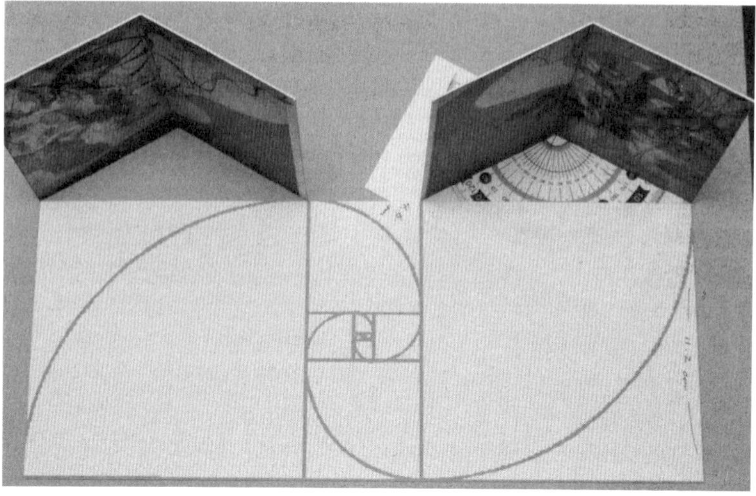

Top view of the silver ratio

size, such as A4 and A3, for example. I myself sometimes use the 1: $(1+\sqrt{2})$ ratio known as the silver rectangle ratio.

When a painting on a set of hinged byobu screens is displayed, the byobu stands on the floor (usually tatami mats) and thus the angle of its folds needs to be considered. Is it a 10-degree fold? A 25-degree fold? Or even more? Depending on the angle, the resulting amount of distortion needs to be taken into consideration and has to be adjusted. This is also true for folding sensu fans. Proper ma and yohaku allow this distortion effect to be minimized and not be too disturbing visually.

Also, one needs to know the light source. For example, does the sunlight (or candlelight, or oil lamp light) come from the right or left? Since both byobu and sensu have their own rules for folding depending on the number of folds and the type, it is important to know that the side facing the light should be prioritized. Both byobu folding screens and fusuma sliding screens are segmented, so because of the framing of the fusuma or the panels of the byobu, you cannot avoid seeing vertical lines dividing the main image.

Sotatsu, *Gods of Wind and Thunder*

Tawaraya Sotatsu

Since most byobu screens are displayed slightly folded, regardless of the number of screens in each set, master painters of Sotatsu's caliber must have considered the distortion that results from folding and used it to their advantage. The ideal way of viewing his byobu may be with consideration of the silver ratio and specific ma space between the two panels. It is important to remember that the painter needs to create a work that looks fine in both conditions: flat without distortion during the process of its creation, and folded with distortion due to the angle of folding as viewed from a seated viewpoint. Most byobu screens are designed to be self-standing so when the screen is folded slightly, it does not require additional support.

For Sotatsu, whether due to tradition or his originality, using gold leaf for the background of his celebrated four-paneled depiction of the wind god, Raijin and thunder god, Fujin, eliminated any need to take background landscape into consideration. The gold-leafed areas function as yohaku, providing space where viewers can breathe and also imagine that they are facing an otherworldly scene. This may give an impression of infinite depth. Also, since the two gods are situated near the edge of the screens, we feel that they have entered the field of view from beyond the frame: Raijin descending diagonally from the left top, and Fujin entering horizontally from the right. They have just arrived on the scene, in a very active manner. Portraying the gods in this particular "ma" enables you to imagine a different dimension, a "godly ma," so to speak. This active but tranquil golden space draws viewers in and is nonthreatening. Each of the gods occupies only two-thirds of its two screens, so they appear to be contained.

Ogata Korin

Korin obviously looked up to Sotatsu, considering him to be his master. Perfect proof of this would be provided by superimposing Korin's screen *Kobai* (Plum Blossoms in Red and White) over Sotatsu's god images with its width to height ratio intact. It is clear that the composition (i.e., spacing/ma between the two figures/trees) is nearly identical. The painting by Korin on the facing page is a prime example of what I have commented on above. His piece appears excellent, in either flat or folded mode, if the same silver ratio is applied. It allows viewers to clearly sense the upper outline of the flowing water. The difference from Sotatsu's composition is that while Sotatsu used gold leaf to express infinity and depth, Korin, by letting water occupy the central section, creates an illusion of expansive continuity toward the viewer. It also allows the viewer to ponder the origin of this onwardly flowing river. As with the byobu by Sotatsu, this image invites us to imagine the world (ma) beyond the frame.

Top right: Sotatsu, *Gods of Wind and Thunder*.
Bottom right: Korin, *Plum Blossoms in Red and White*.

Yohaku and the silver ratio in my own works

Lately, I have started to apply the concepts of Yohaku and the silver ratio to my own creations.

The vertical image *Our Lady of Compassion* (page 102), is the one I have been working on since initially displaying it at The Terminal gallery in Kyoto. The completed version was exhibited at the Kyoto City KYOCERA Museum of Art (formerly the Kyoto Municipal Museum of Art). While I have added a few things, I have narrowed the entire composition to fit the silver ratio. Also, I have added the necessary elements while leaving an ample amount of yohaku or ma space, respecting the original *Hibo-Kannon* image by Kano Hogai. I have been using pre-existing images as Duchampian "ready-mades" in my works, and this one combines elements and themes from both East and West. While Hogai's work focuses on the theme of birth, mine focuses on the ending—death and rebirth.

Whisper

The horizontal painting titled *Whisper* is a digitally created image, applying the silver ratio. It incorporates existing images by Leonardo da Vinci. Yet, instead of cluttering the image as in the Western-style compositions I used to employ, I have placed the central images slightly off-center to match the silver ratio, and as in liubai, I have intentionally left some space not blank but lighter to allow a sense of depth and continuity, so that the viewer can breathe and imagine what could there be.

Marcel Duchamp has stated that an artwork is complete when it is seen by the viewers. By incorporating yohaku, liubai and ma, we enable the viewers to participate in the final stage of the creation process, and thus the true purpose of artistic creation is fulfilled.

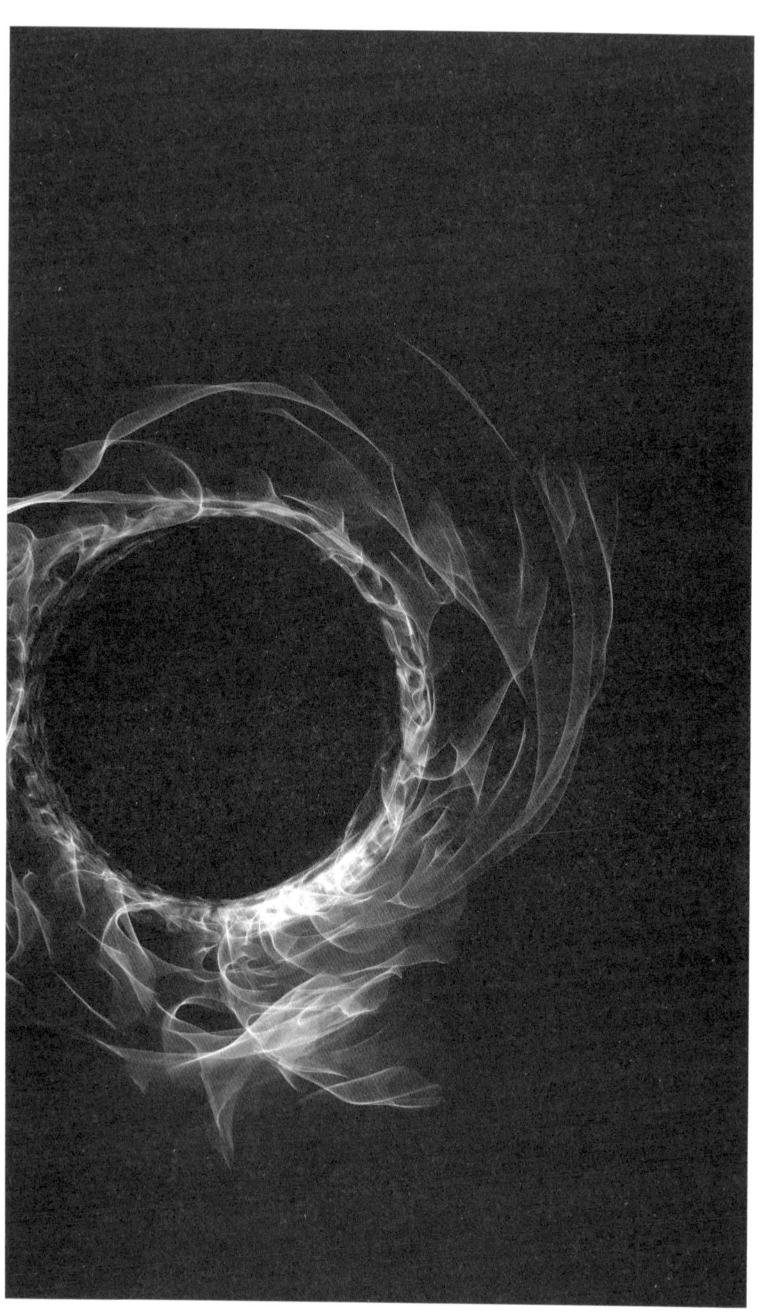

From the series *Tamashi* by Morgan Fisher.

the heart of the matter

translating the Heart Sutra

by Leanne Ogasawara

I BACK IN THE TANG DYNASTY, it was the heart that mattered. Thinking too much, philosophers warned, would only give you a headache. This fact was supported by the finest investigations of Chinese physicians and theologians who urged people to "still their hearts" and "empty their minds" in order to achieve liberation from suffering.

But Chinese Buddhists of the seventh century had a big problem to solve. One that would require some heavy-duty thinking: *how to translate abstract philosophical terms from Sanskrit—a language with an extraordinarily rich epistemological and ontological lexicon—into Chinese, a language poor in abstract vocabulary?*

Words had to be invented. And it wouldn't be easy, for how can a translator know if a translation is correct if they don't have access to the original text?

It was to this task that Xuanzang, the Buddhist monk and translator extraordinaire devoted his life.

II ONE OF THE CORE TEXTS of Mahayana Buddhism, the *Heart Sutra* scarcely fills a page. In English, it is barely 400 words long; in Chinese, a mere 260 characters. A relatively new text, it was written down a thousand years after the Shakyamuni Buddha attained Nirvana. Quickly becoming one of the most widely studied and recited texts in the Mahayana world the *Heart Sutra* is known for the way it pulls the epistemological rug out from beneath our feet. The sutra defies summarization, but its core message is that the outer world is illusory. Nothing is real.

But also, nothing is not real.

Ripping the veil off our preconceived notions, the sutra challenges our understanding of . . . well, of everything. Legend has it that some of Buddha's followers were so perplexed upon first reading it that they suffered heart palpitations!

Even now, two millennia later, people feel confused by the notion that

> FORM IS EMPTINESS, EMPTINESS IS FORM.
> 色不異空。空不異色。

It's a slippery slope notion that attempts to explain a state of existence where nothing comes into being independently. (Got that?) The Chinese language could not cope. And the English language still struggles as well.

For example, how to translate the Sanskrit term *sunyata* (emptiness, voidness zero)? Chinese translators had to proceed with great caution.

Avoiding the obvious choice, no/not/nothing (無), conveying negativity in Chinese, translators instead employed the Chinese word for "sky" (空), suggestive of the "ethers"—like yin and yang—of mist and water, and of energy.

It is "emptiness depending on matter" and "matter depending on emptiness."

Looking out your window, you realize the sky is not "nothing" or "void." Rather, it is a boundless and boundary

-less sphere. The perfect place for birds to fly and clouds to form. A generative space—and this is why some scholars suggest that a better English version of the Chinese translation is:

FORM IS BOUNDLESSNESS, BOUNDLESSNESS IS FORM.

Inseparable. Indivisible. Non-duality.

III IMAGINE A CHINESE LANDSCAPE PAINTING. A gentleman-scholar is gazing across a landscape filled with mist and sky.

There are mountains in the near distance, but the picture is mainly emptiness. The man almost disappears into the empty space. It is a landscape painting, but I would prefer to call it an inner landscape. As if the mind of the viewer, by mirroring the emptiness of the landscape, is thereby able to convey a world in constant flux. Because mountains could not be conceived of without water and mist, the Buddhism-infused landscapes of China and Japan are often filled with a lot of empty space.

Heart is full in inverse relation to an empty mind
Being in the world = the world in being
Emptiness is energy
Invisible energy is visible matter
Yes, $E = mc^2$
Even the cosmic vacuum is full of dark energy . . .

IV DIVIDED FROM THE REST OF THE EMPIRE by tall mountains and deep valleys, the Kingdom of Shu has long been a place of exile, where emperors and kings sent those in disfavor. When the Sui dynasty collapsed in 618, countless numbers of China's famed scholar-artists traveled there as well—either forced or in self-exile. Living in rustic huts, these scholar-artists composed some of the finest poetry and calligraphy in Chinese history.

Among these exiles was Xuanzang, who at sixteen years of age was forced to flee from the capital of Chang'an, with his brother. The two young monks made their way to Chengdu, in the Kingdom of Shu. Here Xuanzang first came into contact with the *Heart Sutra*. Meeting a monk who was sick and hungry, he fed and clothed him, and by way of thanks this monk taught Xuanzang the *Heart Sutra*.

Like the reflective gentleman-scholar in the Chinese painting, surrounded by everything–nothingness, Xuanzang was now a thinker, and he had become concerned about certain discrepancies he had found in religious texts. Many Buddhist sutras and commentaries had been brought from India and translated into Chinese by that time, but Xuanzang understood that the competing interpretations pointed to the real possibility that Chinese monks (himself included!) were not understanding Buddhism in the same way Indians and Central Asians understood it. He committed to joining the ranks of religious pilgrims, and set off to India, where he would study the texts with teachers in the original languages. All this in the hope of attaining real knowledge and deeper truth, on his "Journey to the West."

Statue of Xuanzang.
Photograph by Ken Rodgers.

V Descartes famously began with the idea that "I think, therefore I am." From this idea of mind as the basis of reality, he tentatively derived the outer world as well. There is mind and there is matter. Spirit and substance. And this dualistic way of viewing existence has dominated Western philosophy ever since. The *Heart Sutra* launches this philosophical stance into somersaults . . .

Body is mind, mind is body . . .
One cannot be derived from the other since both are
interdependent.
Everything is interrelated and constantly changing.
Everything is everything else.

The Sanskrit term "emptiness" becomes a double zero. A double negation, the zero that renders everything infinite. A zero that is perfect fullness. Zero over zero (0 / 0) equals infinity. It is:

No eyes, no ears, no nose, no tongue, no body, no mind
No shape, no sound, no smell, no taste, no feeling, no
thought
No this, no that, no nothing, no everything
No path, no heart

VI In Nara, Yakushi Temple has an octagonal hall dedicated to Genjo-Sanzo (as Xuanzang is known in Japan). The hall contains fragments of Xuanzang's relic bones. These were apparently brought back from China by imperial Japanese soldiers stationed in Nanjing in 1942. Above the entrance, there is a sign that reads "No East" (不東) to remind visitors of the monk's strong commitment of heart (決心) to not take even one step back toward home until he had achieved his mission.

And what a mission it was.

Some people consider Xuanzang to be the greatest traveler of all time. Marco Polo perhaps journeyed further in terms of distance—but, well, that was about 450 years later and things were more comfortable then. More importantly, while Polo traveled for reasons of wealth and fame, Xuanzang traveled to find the Truth—to understand the nature of reality, not just for himself—but for the sake of all sentient beings.

Passing through the Anxi Jade Gate in 627, Xuanzang broke imperial regulations by leaving China proper. Traveling west along the Silk Road, he visited many of the ancient Buddhist kingdoms that dotted the path around the edges of the Taklamakam Desert. He made it as far as Afghanistan, where he left record of seeing the great statues of Bamiyan. Then he turned south to India. He almost didn't reach India: so intent was the devout Buddhist King of Turfan to keep the pilgrim living in his kingdom he tried to hold the monk hostage. Rather than from any ill will, the King quite simply could not bear to let such a stimulating conversationalist and brilliant debater leave his realm.

You can hardly blame him, right?

Along the way, Xuanzang was robbed and almost murdered several times, facing great danger again and again. Even a trusted helper turned against him at knifepoint. But Xuanzang had his talisman. In reciting the *Heart Sutra* whenever he was in danger, he kept his resolve and managed to finally make it to Nalanda University, near present-day Patna. This was the great center of Buddhist learning of the time. Xuanzang stayed many years, studying Buddhist philosophy, logic and Sanskrit with the greatest Buddhist teachers of the day. When he returned to China eighteen

Xuanzang statue at Nalanda, Ken Rodgers; at Big Goose Pagoda in Xian, Edward J. Taylor

years later, he hauled a library of books back with him and spent the remainder of his days teaching and translating.

VII XUANZANG'S NEW TRANSLATIONS revolutionized the Chinese Buddhist world. By this time, the emperor had forgiven the monk's unauthorized departure for India and pledged his full support. Some twenty monks were assigned to the translation process—and what a process it was!

Xuanzang first translated the Sanskrit text into spoken Chinese. Then a scribe worked with Xuanzang to transcribe the oral Chinese into Chinese ideograms. Xuanzang's deep experience with Indian Buddhism led to manifold revisions, striving for authenticity. For example, prior to his journey, the land of India was referred to in Chinese as 天竺 (*tianzhu*), from the Chinese transliteration of the Old Persian *hinduka* (Hindu). The ideograms were changed to 印度 (*yìndù*), the default word for "India" in China to this day.

The earlier word for India, 天竺 (*tianzhu*), is still with us today in the modern renditions of the classic Ming dynasty novel *Journey to the West*. This account of Xuanzang's epic journey was made famous in English with the publication of Arthur Waley's abridged translation, titled *Monkey*, which followed the monk on his legendary trip to the land of Tianzhu (Tenjiku in Japanese) with three disciples, including an impetuous monkey with extraordinary magical powers.

After the phonetic step described above, a Sanskrit reader would then confirm the accuracy of Xuanzang's Chinese translation. In the final step, a team member double-checked the ideograms. Many changes were made to further improve the authenticity of the translation. A prominent example was dropping the earlier term for *sattva* (眾生), meaning "multitude of lives or sentient being" and using 有情, which refers to feelings; this would be read as a more precise term when connoting "a sentient being who possesses feelings," 有情 [眾生]. "Sattva" in the Mahayana tradition is a general term for all sentient beings in contrast to buddhas, and Xuanzang's retranslation of this term probably better reflects Mahayana understanding of this core Buddhist concept.

Because of this meticulously attentive multi-step process, Xuanzang's translations are considered to be exceedingly accurate. He was not only the greatest Chinese translator of Sanskrit Buddhist texts of his time, but his translations continue to play a major role to this day—none more than the *Heart Sutra*, for which he is renowned.

VIII Xuanzang's version of the *Heart Sutra* is probably the single-most chanted mantra on earth.

The Sanskrit term for "heart," *hridaya*, means "body, mind, heart . . ." But one other possible meaning for hridaya is "incantation." This has led some scholars to suggest that the sutra was always thought to be fundamentally a mantra. Even now, it is chanted in Buddhist temples daily around the world. In Japan, where it is known as the *Hannya Shingyo*, it is particularly prominent in Rinzai Zen Buddhism. But from Tibet to Japan, the *Heart Sutra* is chanted, read and written with ink and brush as part of the meditation practices of the devout.

The short sutra itself ends with a Great Mantra, explained to be:

The most illuminating mantra,
the highest mantra,
a mantra beyond compare,
the True Wisdom that has the power
to put an end to all kinds of suffering.

This concludes with the incantation

Gate, Gate, Paragate, Parasamgate, Bodhi Svaha!

Meaning, "Gone, gone, everyone gone to the other shore, awakening, Amen."

Or, as Allen Ginsberg translated it: "Gone gone totally gone totally gone over the top, wakened mind, So, ah!"

In 2014, Thich Nhat Hanh, in order to improve Western understanding of the *Heart Sutra*, created a new English translation. He wanted to ensure that no one would ever again misunderstand the sutra in terms of the English word "emptiness." The "zero" or "emptiness" of the Sanskrit term *sunyata* is not a nihilistic teaching, he says. His new title emphasizes the essence of the teaching as one of "inter-being," "no-self," "the middle way," "singleness," and "aimlessness"— *The Insight That Brings Us to the Other Shore.*

We are all drowning in an ocean of *samsara*—of ego, of mis-understandings and mis-translations. If we commit to the *Heart Sutra*, "The Heart of the Perfection of Wisdom," we can use this teaching as a lifeboat—or as Augustine said of Beauty, as "a plank amid the waves of the sea" to paddle toward the Other Shore of Nirvana.

IX HERE'S A QUESTION: Are profound religious truths accessible to people without temple or teacher? Can they arrive in a flash?

Can something appear out of nothing?

Can truth strike you like a lightning bolt in blue skies?

Do mountains smile when all beings open their eyes?

Pointing to a world beyond this one, a storehouse of Buddhist teachings has been passed down generation to generation.

These teachings are embedded in esoteric mandalas and statues of bodhisattvas, and they are chanted by believers daily.

Wisdom beyond wisdom, this is the boundless mind.

That is the grace and beauty of Buddhism—its profound positivity—that each of us is capable, through individual study and practice, of grasping the ultimate reality and achieving liberation.

moments of silence and stillness

Text and photography by Magdalena Rittenhouse

Gates, thresholds, screens and passages—intermediary zones created to gently separate the inside from the outside, the sacred from the profane, the safe and tamed from the unfamiliar.

The kanji character for *ma*, 間, combines 門 "door" and 日 "sun." A door through which beams of sun flow softly into a dark room? The zone where light and shade penetrate each other? An open veranda that is both sheltered and exposed? An intentionally empty *tokonoma* display alcove in a Japanese living room? Or perhaps a screened window—neither transparent nor opaque—which obscures the view of what's beyond, but not quite?

The space in between. Ma enables transitions. It's about dividing and connecting; transcending differences and complexities. It is meant to create moments of silence and stillness.

Ma is the emptiness in which time and space are obliterated, opposites reconciled, thoughts suspended. It is an invitation to awareness.

on isolation

Text and photography by Kit Pancoast Nagamura

I

Photographers, much like poets and artists, do a lot of work alone. Isolation, metaphysically at least, is a landscape we know, explore, and at times get lost in. Even on crowded trains and city streets, and despite social network sites, ubiquitous TV, traffic, and de rigueur personal interactions at work, we can ironically *feel* isolated. But encountering true physical distancing—when there's not a soul around as far as the eye can see—can give us a tingle of trepidation.

When I spotted this *torii* gate (see pages 20–21 of photographic insert), suggesting a shrine further up in the mountains, I knew exploring it on my own held some minor risks. It was the throbbing hot center of summer. I was suffering a minor leg injury, and had only a half-bottle of water with me. I had left a deserted town below, and climbed without seeing a soul to a series of abandoned rice fields. There could be snakes. There were surely mosquitos. And I was already out of cellphone range.

I redistributed my cameras, and continued up. The day held the kind of heat where cicada song vibrates in every bead of your sweat, and the essence of the mountain itself vaporizes, so that you suck in its black-green essence with each breath. By the time I reached the lichen-covered stone torii, I felt mildly delirious. Beyond the entrance, the shade of the trees was so dark my eyes fought to focus. I took a few pictures there, and though I know how to shoot in low light, the shots turned out blurred beyond mere incompetence, like photos of ghosts.

Beyond the torii, there was a path heading upward, which I climbed and climbed, wiping away curtains of thick spider webs, and every now and then, I would stop for water, and to listen to the strange sphere of sound made by insects. I crossed a river, and headed upward again, the thump of my heart in each step. Eventually, after an hour, I realized that there might be no shrine to arrive at, no clearing in the woods or marked paths to choose. The shrine, I finally realized, could well be simply the mountain itself.

Later, heading down the mountain again and past the overgrown and abandoned rice terraces, I turned to look back at the gate. The afternoon was full of cabbage butterflies in the slanted sunlight, and the air had the odor of baked grasses. I could see the mountain's shape, forming the kanji character for mountain, and a single cloud coalescing into a focal point above. Here is the holiness you might find in isolation, I thought, and I prayed to it.

a clap
becoming a mountain
cloud

II

Every day you were heading in one direction, following some flow your life had taken on, barely noticing that the accumulation of days had carved a canyon in which you found yourself, rushing forward, with no time to ask: is this sustainable? Then a landslide hit. Some things got buried, others damaged in a scrabble of rocks or ruined in slippery mud. Some things were swept away. Your path is at the moment blocked, but a pool of water fills again, slowly, with time. Without the usual movement, your familiar tumble downstream between worn banks, you might feel, as the water level rises, that you could drown in yourself. But brimming is on the way, when the water's dome of surface tension will rise and catch light. From there the water might break out in any direction because decisions, perhaps your first in a long time, are imminent.

III

stay at home decree
the indoor cat eyes me
full of knowing

virtual meetings
every emotion broken
into pixels

IV

International borders have been sealed tight. I spend some time traveling through photos of my birthplace. I pause at a series I shot a year earlier, of spathes, or deciduous sheathes that isolate and protect a palm tree's inflorescence from outside dangers until the flowers are ready to emerge. I try to take comfort in the pearlescent interiors of these large spathes, the size of baby cradles, fallen from Roystonea palms. Instead, staring at their linear dark interiors, and curved curtains, their sinewy enclosing structure makes my brow sweat with claustrophobia. I leave the images to research Roystoneas, commonly known as Royal Palms. I learn they were named for Roy Stone, a Union Army officer in the US Civil War who later was instrumental in road-building projects, and credited with the invention of the steam monorail.

I hop that train of thought instead.

V

What day of the week is it, again? Does it matter? What if we stay up until 4:00 a.m.? Is every 4:00 a.m. an ethereal blue like this, a glorious glassy hour we usually sleep right through? How long can we stay in PJs, and does the Sagawa Kyubin delivery guy's grin mean he likes our PJs? What did we have for lunch, or did we have lunch, and wait a minute . . . why are we talking to ourselves in the third person? We don't care. It's probably normal. We are not going nuts. We have to admit, though, that we should clean up our house, but we cannot, which is too bad because if we could, we might fool ourselves into thinking we were sheltering in a brand new place. Instead, between news broadcasts, we weep at TV commercials with family reunions. We bake. We grow something.

We grow fat. We read books that have been waiting so long their spines are weak. We exercise so our spines don't go weak. We find we don't spend much money in isolation, we just don't. Unless we touch the Internet, and order things we've never ordered before. We order so much the Sagawa Kyubin man feels like family. And this is bad because finances are uncertain right now. We are on edge. We roll our eyes. We roll and spin in bed, because we

know there is something important we are not doing. We know we shouldn't waste such odd precious time alone. We've tried writing journals, letters, using up all the old stationery in the house. We've tried virtual book clubs, and we've wiled away the hours in the cardboard of games and hobbies and puzzles. But we ache for casual contact, for the kismet of skinship. Is life worth living without the sudden embrace from a neighbor's child, the high-five of a colleague who got her raise, the intimacy of pouring wine for a cluster of friends? We think, what did we do to deserve this isolation? We think we know the answer to that question. When it all ends, will we change what we are doing wrong? Or will we not? How will we look back on these days when we stayed inside, and outside we heard, as if for the first time, the sound of birds, singing and singing?

VI

outside again
bending to the summer grasses
from a dream

the deadly dance of distance

Text and photography by Alexander Bennett

A timeless piece of wisdom in Japanese martial arts says, "Victory lies in understanding *ma-ai*." From the moment I first stepped into a kendo dojo and picked up a *shinai* bamboo practice sword, this principle was woven into every lesson, quietly shaping the foundation of my practice.

The term *ma* refers to time, distance or space. Combined with *ai*, it translates to "meeting the ma," a concept that encompasses timing, distancing and spatial adjustment. Mastering the precise distance to deliver an attack with maximum impact, while maintaining perfect balance and posture, is essential in *budo*, the Japanese martial ways.

Each budo art offers its own perspective on ma-ai, shaped by whether weapons are involved and the lengths of those weapons, yet the core principles remain universal. Because every practitioner's physique, height and reach are different, there is always some variation, often down to the smallest measurement. The aim is to avoid being too close, which increases mutual risk, or too far, which makes effective attacks impossible. The ideal ma-ai is "comfortably reachable" for you while feeling "uncomfortably unreachable" for your opponent. By creating this sense of unease, you push your adversary onto the back foot, seizing control of the encounter—much like a conductor dictating the tempo of an orchestra.

In other words, mastering your own ma-ai is as much about psychology as it is about physicality. Closing in on your ideal striking distance with confidence and clear intent can unnerve your opponent, forcing them onto the defensive and disrupting their composure. If you can provoke such a response, you've already tilted the odds significantly in your favor—even before making the decisive blow.

This isn't about rushing in recklessly, though. Far from it. Accurately reading, adjusting and managing ma-ai is one of the most demanding skills in any budo practice, requiring years of diligent refinement. You must know exactly when and how far to move forward, when to step back, and how to strike with impeccable timing and distance to achieve maximum effectiveness. Get too close, and your strike will lack power. Stay too far away, and it either won't reach or will be weak. At the same time, you must read your opponent's distance so precisely that you can avoid their attack by the narrowest margin—perhaps a hair's breadth.

Ma-ai is fluid, changing with your experience, skill and age. Yet, in the end, the practitioner who controls their ma-ai controls the fight. In a text from the illustrious Itto-ryu school of swordsmanship, this concept is explained succinctly and is as relevant now in the modern budo arts as it was when samurai swordsmen engaged in life-or-death duels:

> The essence of victory lies in ma-ai. When you seek to gain an advantage, so too will your opponent. If you move forward, your opponent will inevitably respond. The pivotal factor in victory or defeat resides within this ma-ai. The concept of *ma-zumori*—passed down in our tradition—refers to incrementally closing the distance in harmony with rhythm and cadence. When confronting an opponent, do not permit even

the slightest opening within this ma-ai. Without hesitation and undeterred by danger, boldly seize the initiative and strike. By mastering the precise balance between life and death in the moment of engagement, one can disrupt the opponent's position and gain complete control. (*Ittosai-sensei Kenposho,* 1664)

Ma-ai embodies a dynamic interplay, often expressed through traditional concepts like "*Shin, Gyo, So no ma-ai*" (Precision, Fluidity, Intuition intervals) or the "three levels of ma-ai." These include *issoku-itto-no-ma* (one-step, one-sword interval), *to-ma* (distant interval), *chika-ma* (close interval), as well as the extremely tight *seriai-no-ma* (grappling interval).

Even the fundamental issoku-itto-no-ma is not a rigid standard. It varies based on factors like physique, stance, skill level, weapon length and situational conditions. For example, practitioners skilled at lunging often favor a longer distance, while those with less agility may find a closer range advantageous. Everybody has their own

石橋

optimal ma-ai, just as their opponent does. In this sense, ma-ai shifts according to individual strengths and weaknesses. For this reason, it is essential for practitioners learn to identify and operate within the ma-ai that aligns with their capabilities, ensuring they maintain an advantage in any encounter.

Achieving this demands a flawless integration of footwork, weapon handling, and, most critically, mastery of ma-ai. These elements must work together fluidly, allowing you to adapt to the opponent's every move and establish a favorable position. By maintaining an advantageous distance and skillfully probing the opponent's vulnerable spaces, you can take command of the encounter. Such moments are often likened to "a cat stalking the wind"—a vivid image of inevitability, where victory feels as though it was always within reach.

This idea is captured in the saying, "The sword that enters ma-ai lives, while the sword that allows the opponent to enter ma-ai perishes." This paradox points to a deeper truth: in budo, ma-ai encompasses not only the tangible aspects of footwork, distance control, and the positioning of the weapon's tip, be that of a fist or a sword, but also the intangible, nuanced dynamics of the mind.

This "mental ma-ai" involves sensing the opponent's intentions, maintaining an unshakable calm, and subtly suppressing their movements while plaiting together both physical and psychological strategies. Mastering this delicate balance of the seen and unseen is what defines the essence of true ma-ai.

Ma-ai is thus far more than just a measure of distance; it is the heartbeat of any encounter in martial arts, blending precision, timing, and psychological insight. To master ma-ai is to master control—over yourself, your opponent, and the flow of the fight. It demands constant refinement, as no two encounters are ever the same, and every movement is an opportunity to assert dominance or expose vulnerability. Whether on the battlefield of the past or in the modern dojo, ma-ai remains the cornerstone of martial arts.

constructing reality

VR and the formless mind

A dialog between Atticus Sims and the Rev. Takafumi Kawakami
all images by Atticus Sims

Consciousness is one of the great mysteries of life, and in modern times researchers and philosophers alike have struggled to make significant progress in uncovering the mechanisms that caused its emergence in life on our planet.

Buddhists have been exploring the subjective nature of consciousness for millennia through meditation, while the recent emergence of immersive technologies such as virtual reality (VR) have given us the opportunity to gain insight into our consciousness by allowing us to interact within novel simulated worlds that can be starkly different from the physical world of everyday experience. Both of these may help to reveal a space beyond the reality of our ordinary awareness that can provide some insight into how to better navigate the complexities of life today.

ATTICUS SIMS: VR has been described positively as the ultimate empathy machine, and the final medium. Conversely, it's been called the perfectly evil Skinner box, in that creators of virtual worlds can programmatically limit choices and reward behaviors of participants to a much greater extent than that of other media such as smart phones or traditional gaming consoles. I believe VR is the truest one can get to directly sharing one's mind with another. It does this by substituting real world sensory inputs of vision, sound and, potentially, touch, smell and taste, with those created by other minds. In this conversation, I'd like to investigate the impact and potential of VR primarily through the lens of a Buddhist perspective of consciousness, perception, and the nature of reality. To begin, I'd like to ask about your perspective on VR.

TAKAFUMI KAWAKAMI: First of all, my perspective is that while we see VR technology getting more sophisticated, at this point it's very primitive, with goggles displaying visual stimuli with audio stimuli and in some cases haptic feedback, but it's not a whole-body experience. Even though we can have a sense of realism in VR, it presents a smaller amount of information. One example is studies about whether subjects can remember more using physical books versus digital books such as Kindle. The results to date indicate that it's physical books, but we don't know for sure because it may be simply that many subjects have grown up with physical books. But for me, when I try to recall information from books, I'm not just visually picturing, or logically just remembering. I might recall I was holding the book and its left-hand side was a little heavier, so what I'm looking for is in this part of the book. In this way I think VR at the moment is really limited in that there is limited information provided.

It is like the hypersonic effect. To record music on a CD we only record the audible sound, eliminating sounds inaudible to the human ear. For instance, if you are wearing noise-canceling ear muffs, your body is still perceiving some sound in the inaudible zone, and your brain is still reacting. So, our whole body is experiencing something all the time. It's not just limited to the visual information or audio information that we recognize consciously. There are more things we are experiencing at the subconscious level.

AS: Research indicates that our brains make decisions well before we are aware of doing so. In experiments where subjects were given a decision-making task, researchers were able to use brain activity to accurately predict choices up to ten seconds prior to the subjects' conscious decisions. This shows that there are all kinds of things going on beneath the surface of what we perceive as our conscious reality, and these insights may provide us with tools that can help us to more effectively engage with the world we experience.

One of the founding fathers of VR, Jaron Lanier, talks about VR as a sort of ongoing investigation that results in a better understanding of what is real. Rather than a substitute for physicality, or "real" reality, Lanier talks about VR as a tool for pushing our consciousness to become better at distinguishing what is real. In any form of digital media, there's always going to be a gap between what is really real and what is simulated, as our bodies have evolved for millions of years to be attuned to what is there in the physical world. Lanier says in his book, *Dawn of the New Everything,* that "a coarser simulated reality fosters appreciation for the depth of physical reality in comparison. As VR progresses in the future, human perception will be nurtured by it, and it will learn to find ever more depth in physical reality."

TK: There is an idea in Eastern philosophy that we should not focus too much on explicit knowledge—intellectual understanding and rational thinking—but rather on tacit knowledge. For example, Taoism emphasizes learning from action rather than from words.

Master craftsmen say that when they train apprentices, they can teach 80 to 90 percent of the trade by giving instruction, but the last 10 to 20 percent they have to learn through their bodies. By observing the teacher and copying, they come to know the skill in an embodied way. Some craftsmen talk about possibly using VR to create similar experiences, but the issue is that everyone's body is different. Everyone has different sizes of hands and different densities of nerve endings in their hands, so what one person feels differs significantly from the next person, even with the same stimuli.

On some levels, as humans we react in the same ways universally to certain things, but many mindfulness-based interventions, for instance, do not work well for certain groups. The definition of well-being used in the World Happiness Report is based on universalism—everybody behaves the same way or reacts the same. There have been mindfulness-based interventions created to improve well-being for organizations, but in these cases, whose well-being are we talking about? The field of well-being is now dominated by researchers from a Western, Educated, Industrialized, Rich Democratic background, or WEIRD people, and it's possible that their ideas of well-being don't work for the majority of the world.

So how do we overcome this? Everybody has a different response in the same situation, so how are we going to create a universal solution whether in the field of well-being or in VR?

AS: One thing I saw when I first tried VR was the possibility for this type of physical training. The traditional way of learning a craft in Japan is to practice for ten years, because knowledge has to be really embodied before you can master a skill. The potential I see in simulations is even though you can't do the real thing, you get certain types of feedback from various sensors, creating a bridge between tacit and explicit understanding. A craftsperson could learn basic movements, and if paired with the embodied experience of actually doing the thing, the type of feedback that you can get is quite valuable and something that might be difficult to get elsewhere.

To intellectualize something is to take it out of its form as pure experience and create an abstraction of it. We can parse that abstraction and manipulate it with language, which helps a certain form of understanding. This type of conceptualization is useful to analyze and share ideas through language, but there are certain aspects of consciousness that are only knowable through direct experience. To me, from my firsthand glimpses from meditation, it seems there's a boundless continuum of awake awareness that serves as the ground of all of our conscious experiences. I think most people today identify fully with their thoughts and maintain the sense of being an observer located inside their head, looking out into the world. I believe that recognizing this and learning to shift one's perspective into what we might call the formless mind is important in many ways.

TK: Zen Buddhism has been called anti-intellectual, but this doesn't mean that the use of the intellect is meaningless. No matter what we do, we conceptualize what we experience, and we do so instantaneously. Once a concept has been created in our heads we pay attention to the concept and not the thing that's being experienced. I think this is human nature. Japanese Zen master Sogen Omori said fire is hot for anyone, anywhere and at any time. But that is just our concept of fire and not the fire in front of you. For human beings it is much easier to live using concepts than to pay attention to what's actually happening, because it's simplified and we can emphasize the part that we want to hear or see. So, it's a matter of convenience for the one that is perceiving.

AS: Buddhism is sometimes considered a proto-science of consciousness. If you look Zen or other meditation-based traditions such as Dzogchen of Tibetan Buddhism, they've had very complex and broad views of the nature of consciousness, reality and our perceptions. Can you go into more detail about the Buddhist description of reality in terms of our senses and consciousness?

TK: First, I think we should be careful about using the term "reality." There's a difference between "reality" and "actuality," or in Buddhist terms delusion and dharma. In philosophical terms, reality is our image of actuality, or truth, and it is something we create based on what we perceive and the concepts in our heads. Kant says that truth exists independent of human consciousness and human experience, but as long as we are human we cannot perceive truth as it actually is, and the realities we create in our minds and our images of truth influence our behaviors, which in turn influence truth.

According to some Buddhist traditions, if you train more you see things more as they are in actuality, but, at the same time, there is a limit to our nature as human beings. This is not unique to Buddhism; it is found in Judaism, Islam or Christianity. Most religions say that as humans we cannot perceive truth or the will of the higher being the way it truly is because their existence is beyond the human imagination. In Hinduism there is Brahma, in Judaism there is Yahweh, in Islam there is Allah and in Buddhism we have the dharma, and none of these can be perceived completely by a human being.

AS: One of the key practices in Buddhism is the observation of the senses in order to comprehend the nature of *Dhukka*, or suffering. It is interesting that there are considered to be six senses in Buddhism: sight, hearing, smell, taste and bodily sensations with the addition of thought. So there are five inputs from outside our bodies and then thought as a sense which is generated internally.

TK: The classic question in the book, *Zen and the Art of Motorcycle Maintenance* is: if you are born without any functioning sense organs, can you develop consciousness? If from birth you cannot see anything, you cannot hear anything, you have no smell, no taste and no kinetic sensation that can be used to form your consciousness, the Buddhist answer to the question is probably no, but in Western philosophy the answer is yes. Western philosophy believes in an independent self, originating in the notion of mind–body dualism started by Plato and then refined by Descartes. The Buddhist idea of self is that you need to have a body, and you need to have sense-gates. The self is interdependent, and it is also impermanent. That idea is important because there's this impermanent body surrounded by a physical or social environment, and the interactions between them create reactions. Those are sensations and feelings that actually create mental activity like thinking. So, the Buddhist way of looking at the world is that if we don't have any sense organs, then there are no reactions, and consciousness cannot form.

AS: We seem to have an intuitive sense of what self is, but when you really start to dig into it, whether from a more analytical perspective, or just through observation and through insight meditation, it becomes very tricky to say whether or not there is a self.

TK: Maybe self actually exists but for me the more dominant idea is that the self is interdependent. During meditation, while observing my feelings, sensations and mental activities, I also think about what is conscious and what is not conscious. Consciously, I'm recognizing how my body is functioning, my reactions, my reflexes and so on. But where is my mind? Where is my consciousness? It points to the space in-between. This is the Buddhist notion of emptiness. Emptiness doesn't mean that this is an empty void. People use that word, but it's not void. It's the connections, relationships, interactions—that is what is meant by emptiness. It's not like there is a self there, but there is interaction. As my meditation practice deepens, the more I feel this way.

That's the reason talking about VR is interesting, because it is something that provides the possibility for certain interactions.

AS: Norbert Wiener, a seminal figure in the birth of computing, created the theoretical framework called cybernetics, which he defined as "the scientific study of control and communication in the animal and the machine." In his book about cybernetics written for a lay audience, *The Human Use of Human Beings,* he presents dire warnings regarding the potential consequences of his own work that presage the present world we live in, where humans all too often are treated as machines. But his analysis of the role of feedback in systems, whether mechanical or biological, led him to view our interconnectedness—not only to one another but to all life—as fundamental. He states, "we are not the stuff that abides, but patterns that perpetuate themselves," which seems to me to support the Buddhist idea of self as interdependence.

I believe that VR offers us the potential to experience our consciousness or awareness in this way. Going back to Jaron Lanier, he says that VR lets you feel your consciousness in its pure form: "There you are, the fixed point in a system where everything else can change." In VR you can change your identity where you can be a cloud, a mouse, an angel, a stone or an octopus. You can have four legs and three arms, you can have no body or a huge body or you can be someone of the opposite sex. Simulations provided by this technology are real enough for the user to be convinced of the illusion at least temporarily, but it causes one to really wonder: What is this? What is real? What is consciousness? Who am I?

As I began practicing meditation at a deeper level, I began pondering similar questions, and this led me to inquire about the overlap between meditation and convincingly real simulated realities. When spending time in VR, especially when you're creating VR, you begin to notice whenever you leave the simulation that your ability to really look deeply at the physical world and your sensory phenomenon is enhanced. You usually look at something and automatically say, for example, "that's a glass." But if you look at a glass in a simulation and then look at a glass in the real world you begin to notice more about it, you notice how the edges are maybe not completely well defined, or you might notice the reflections on the glass and how they interplay with the light. And from these insights I believe that these immersive technologies may be able to help people explore some of the fundamental issues that Buddhism addresses.

TK: At the same time, I think a good point is that we can't really understand whether we are responding to something or merely reacting, and I think it's difficult to know what we are consciously acknowledging and what we are processing at the unconscious level that might be influencing our conscious decisions or responses.

Going back to the idea of the hypersonic effect, the things that we thought are not important are actually important. With VR we need to think about what the important elements are that make humans react in one way or another to certain stimuli. A scary part of VR is to consider who's making the decisions about what is important for people to experience. Who's making the formula? I think that's going to be a huge issue.

As mentioned in the beginning, VR can be good or it can be bad. But people today never question things. People say, "The Bible says this, and that's why I'm acting this way," or, "Science says this, it's scientifically approved so I'm doing this." People like this can be negatively influenced by VR as things become more sophisticated. But people who have humility and curiosity, who observe themselves, inquiring about what they can learn, about what causes their reactions, for these people it doesn't matter if it's VR or what they are already experiencing, there's no difference.

photographic ma

Text and photography by Robert van Koesveld

When my Japanese friends use the word *ma*, they usually bracket its use with a verbal or nonverbal gesture that says "don't ask me more about the word . . . I just know it when I see it." Interestingly, this applies to both photographers and non-photographers.

Photographers speak about "composition," using words like balance, tension, empty space, leading lines, relative weight. But if an image is to have a chance at communicating something complex, subtle or mysterious, then it needs *spaces* inside it that draw in the unconscious mind, the unknowing mind, the feeling self. Gestures that touch you lighter than a feather or reach out from the void like a scream. Or a whisper. Is that a form of ma?

Appropriating a word from a language you don't know is fraught, of course. But the promise of finding something that might communicate that which has been unnameable till now is seductive. If I surrender to that sort of seduction, I might describe it as a *gestalt*. All the elements coming together, including context and presentation, in a way that invites a subjective response. A space for the heart.

Robert van Koesveld is an Australian photographer/psychotherapist. His exhibition work focuses on the quality of presence, timelessness, and the liminal world located between past and present, personal and archetypal, day-to-day and sacred. His photo books include *Geiko & Maiko of Kyoto.*

Photograph by John Einarsen.

finding the sky

by Michael Dylan Welch

There's a story about Tibetan Buddhist master Chögyam Trungpa Rinpoche that speaks to the idea of implication in haiku. In 1971, Rinpoche was teaching a class on Buddhism at the University of Colorado. In one lecture, as John J. Baker reports in his article, "The Dharma in a Single Drawing" (*Tricycle*, Spring 2015), Rinpoche drew a picture on the blackboard, and asked, "What is this a picture of?" Eventually someone answered by saying the obvious, "It's a picture of a bird," as indeed it was. But Rinpoche then said something that altered his students' view of the obvious, akin to how we might approach haiku. He said, "It's a picture of the sky."

A lesson for haiku poets is we can fixate so intensely on what's in front of us that we neglect what is out the corner of the eye, what might be happening at the same time, and what might be implied—emotionally, culturally and spatially. As readers, too, we can focus so much on the image that we miss its context, again usually implied. It's one thing to think about the Japanese concept of *ma*, or the silence or psychological space within the poem, usually created by *kireji* in Japanese haiku, but another challenge to think about the "space" *around* the poem as well. Kireji are "cutting words" that divide haiku into two juxtaposed parts, both grammatically and imagistically separate. At first seemingly unrelated, these two parts interact much like a chemical reaction—like the mixing of baking soda and vinegar. Kazue Mizumura refers to kireji as "soul punctuation," as "virtually untranslatable emotional shading." They give the reader two parts to leap between, and create a transcendent space within the poem. But more than that, an effective haiku has space around these two parts as well, making one plus one equal three.

The poem's emotional effect is perhaps the most obvious consequence of the words we read, something deeper than superficial compassion we might feel in a haiku about a puppy or homeless person. A broader compassion recognizes that the subject in the poem *matters*, whatever it is, moving beyond a feeling of "This is wonderful" or "This is sad" to the exclamation "This is." We direct this sense of wonder to the particular focus of each poem, and to the relationship we and the author have to each individual subject. An additional context is whatever we may know about the author. For example, we know Shiki's short life was wracked with pain from tuberculosis, which provides a profound emotional context for many of his poems. This is part of the space around the poem.

Culturally, the poem shares a moment of experience in our language, in our time, with allusions to the places, events and activities of our daily lives. Part of the space we might bring to a poem is knowing when it was written, and who it was written for. For example, if a haiku refers to "tending the fire," such a reference two centuries ago would readily imply a fireplace or stove, which would have been the only source of heat in many homes. This context makes tending a fire a chore, a necessity. But when tending a fire today, in our comfortable lives, we might think of camping, or as a luxury in a chiefly decorative fireplace at home, thus a choice rather than a chore. Thus, the meaning of the poem would be affected by the context of when it was written, not just in terms of what wars were being fought at the time, but in much simpler matters of language. The cultural space around a poem is an intuitive exercise in empathy and sometimes projection, but other implications—the skies around the birds—are less obvious.

Indeed, aside from the effect of haiku's "fourth line" (the context provided by the name under the poem), and the way meaning might change over time, the seasoned haiku reader takes a moment to contemplate other factors that provide context for the poem. No wonder Seisensui referred to haiku as an "unfinished" poem, requiring the reader's interaction to complete the poem's scant details, to extrapolate the context, what might happen next, and the emotional or cultural setting of each poem. In Cor van den Heuvel's famous "tundra" poem, the white space around the word, alone in the middle of the otherwise blank page, provides an example of one kind of spatial context—with so little text that one has to interact with the poem to "finish" it. Here the "snow" around the "rock" of the word "tundra," as if emerging from snow melting in the spring, can imply space and expanse, with a hint of spring's promise of resurgence after a bleak and barren winter. This is not the most important kind of spatial implication, however. In *The Way of Zen* (Pantheon, 1957), Alan Watts wrote that "In poetry the empty space is the surrounding silence . . . of the mind in which one does not 'think about' the poem but actually feels the sensation which it evokes—all the more strongly for having said so little." Indeed, in more conventional haiku, a different kind of spatial implication occurs when we think of what else is happening in the context of the poem in front of us—the environment that is part of the poem's "space." Consider this poem by Peggy Willis Lyles:

> winter night
> he patiently untangles
> her antique silver chain

Spatially, in a physical sense, we can imagine an implied wife, perhaps in the next room, waiting just as patiently—or perhaps not even aware that her husband is helping to solve a problem for her. The *kigo* or seasonal reference tells us something, too. Long, dark winter evenings provide the time to focus on tasks like this. The question a sensitive reader will ask is "what is this poem about?" The obvious answer is the untangling of a silver chain. But the deeper answer is relationships, probably between a husband and wife, and the love one feels for the other, demonstrated by the patient untangling of an heirloom that is now the wife's, but surely has a much longer history. It is, after all, an antique chain. So really the poem is about relationships over generations, about the "chain" of connections from person to person that motivated a mother to give the silver chain to her daughter, and for that daughter to give it to her daughter—and how family members near these mothers and daughters are also part of the heirloom's history. While the chain of connections may become tangled over the decades, we still seek to untangle and understand them. This is because we value them, and the love, history and continuity they represent—added to here by the attention demonstrated by the husband who values his wife even more than the symbolic value of a prized possession.

Yes, sensitive haiku readers will ask, "What is this poem really about?" In the best haiku, the answer is not what's in plain sight. The more sensitive answer is akin to saying "It's a picture of the sky." It's our job as haiku readers to discover each poem's sky.

Postscript 1

In *Haiku Mind* (Shambhala, 2008), Patricia Donegan presents this poem in the chapter "Sky Mind." She says it was "Allen Ginsberg's death haiku, written about a week before he died":

To see Void vast infinite
look out the window
into the blue sky.

Donegan adds the following commentary:

> This haiku is a wonderful reminder of a simple practice in the Tibetan Buddhist tradition called sky meditation: looking up into the vast sky and feeling the large expanse of space, which stops our mind's preoccupation of the moment. The sky is merely a reminder of this openness that is always within us, that we can tap into anytime. Wherever we are, we can always simply stop and look up at the sky, or even imagine the sky . . . and breathe out a long-awaited sigh. For a moment we are back to our natural state of mind, which is as vast and open as the sky; all else is just thoughts and feelings like clouds passing by. In any moment we can come back to sky mind.

Ginsberg's poem first appeared in *Death & Fame: Last Poems 1993–1997* (HarperFlamingo, 1999). To me it's more of a statement than a haiku, but Donegan explains that it is an "American Sentence," Ginsberg's alternative to haiku, just seventeen syllables, usually in one line. But still it's a sky mind poem, and seeking sky mind may be part of what it means to find the sky in each haiku we write and read.

Postscript 2

I recently came across these words from a meditation exercise in John Brehm's *The Dharma of Poetry* (Wisdom Publications, 2021):

> In this meditation . . . practice noticing the space between and around everything. Just as we are conditioned to focus on our thoughts, rather than the space between thoughts, we are conditioned to focus on objects rather than the space between them. Shifting the focus of our outward visual attention from things to space can help us detach from thoughts and relax into awareness itself.

Indeed, as any experienced downhill skier will tell you, the secret to skiing well through a glade of trees is not to look at the trees but at the spaces between them.

Contributors

Alexandre Avdulov is an Associate Professor of Japanese language and culture at the Department of Languages and Cultures at Saint Mary's University in Halifax, Canada. He has studied, practiced, and taught tea ceremony since 1983. He is a co-founder of Yukoan teahouse and study group in Halifax, Nova Scotia, Canada.

Alexander Bennett is Vice President of the International Naginata Federation, Director of the Japanese Academy of Budo, and Head Coach of the NZ Kendo national team. His books include *Bushido: The Samurai Code of Japan* and *Hagakure, Kendo: Culture of the Sword.*

Edward A. Burger is a documentary filmmaker. His film *The Mountain Path: My Search for a Hermit Zen Master in China* records conversations with Chinese Buddhist hermits.

Michael Dylan Welch founded National Haiku Writing Month. He was keynote speaker for the Haiku International Association in Tokyo, and his poems, essays and reviews have appeared in hundreds of journals and anthologies. graceguts.com.

Hikaru Hirata-Miyakawa lives in Kyoto where he practices his art and continues his long-time research on Leonardo da Vinci. His desire to understand Leonardo inspired him to become an artist, as shared in his TEDx Talk (Boulder, 2015). Through appreciation of the beauty of Kyoto, he is now turning his gaze back to his roots.

Mark Hovane curates Kyoto Garden Experience to share Japan's rich landscape heritage with garden lovers around the world. Originally from Australia, he lives in Kyoto and has been fascinated by empty spaces since childhood. www.kyotogardenexperience.com

Pico Iyer has published 17 books, translated into 23 languages, including bestsellers *The Art of Stillness, The Half Known Life* and *Aflame.* His five talks for TED have received more than 11 million views so far.

The Rev. Takafumi Kawakami is deputy abbot of Shunko-in Temple in Kyoto. He teaches mindfulness and Zen to international audiences and is involved with many projects that bridge traditional and modern, including collaboration with Keio Media Design and the development of smartphone apps for mindfulness. shunkoin.com

Alex Kerr came to Japan as a child in 1964. Starting with an old thatched house he bought in 1973, he has restored 50 houses around Japan. His books on Japanese art and landscape include *Lost Japan*

(Penguin, 1996), *Another Kyoto* (Penguin, 2016), and *Hidden Japan* (Tuttle, 2024).

Stephen Mansfield is a writer and photographer whose work has appeared in over 100 magazines, newspapers and journals. He is the author of *Japanese Stone Gardens* (Tuttle, 2017); *Japan's Master Garden* (Tuttle, 2018); *100 Japanese Gardens* (Tuttle, 2019); and *The Modern Japanese Garden* (Thames & Hudson, 2025).

John McGee has studied, practiced and taught tea ceremony since 1971. He is co-founder of Yukoan tea house and study group in Halifax, Nova Scotia Canada. He teaches Japanese at Saint Mary's University, Halifax, Canada.

Gunter Nitschke wrote *The Architecture of the Japanese Garden* (Taschen, 1991) and *From Shinto to Ando—Studies in Architectural Anthropology in Japan*, (Academy Editions,1993). He is Director of the Institute for East Asian Architecture and Urbanism in Kyoto. This essay originated as a Cornell University talk in 1976. It was published in *Kyoto Journal* #8, 1988, and in *From Shinto to Ando*.

Leanne Ogasawara has worked as a translator from Japanese for over twenty years, in the fields of academia, poetry, philosophy, and documentary film. She has been contributing to *Kyoto Journal* for twenty years—from poetry translations to interviews to articles.

Kit Pancoast Nagamura is the author of photo-journalism column, "The Backstreet Stories," in *The Japan Times*, has appeared on NHK World's *Journeys in Japan*, and was co-host of NHK World's *Haiku Masters* for three years. Her latest book of haiku is *Grit, Grace, and Gold* (Kodansha, 2020).

Joshua Pearl lived in Kyoto from 1987–1994. He founded the annual Crosscurrents concert series, studied koto under Sawako Fukuhara and jazz piano under Sadayasu Fuji, and was musical coordinator for the 1993 Kyoto Global Forum of Spiritual and Parliamentary Leaders. He works as a clinical music therapist in Portland, Oregon. joshuapearlmusictherapy.com.

Magdalena Rittenhouse is a writer and photographer whose work focuses on nature and the built environment. She is currently based in New York, but left her heart in Kyoto. magdarittenhouse.com

Atticus Sims, an artist and researcher, specializes in AI and immersive technologies. In 2016, he founded Kyoto VR, a studio dedicated to preserving Kyoto's cultural heritage through immersive media. His work is informed by meditation practice and Buddhist perspectives on consciousness. atticussims.com

"Books to Span the East and West"

Tuttle Publishing was founded in 1832 in the small New England town of Rutland, Vermont [USA]. Our core values remain as strong today as they were then—to publish best-in-class books which bring people together one page at a time. In 1948, we established a publishing outpost in Japan—and Tuttle is now a leader in publishing English-language books about the arts, languages and cultures of Asia. The world has become a much smaller place today and Asia's economic and cultural influence has grown. Yet the need for meaningful dialogue and information about this diverse region has never been greater. Over the past seven decades, Tuttle has published thousands of books on subjects ranging from martial arts and paper crafts to language learning and literature—and our talented authors, illustrators, designers and photographers have won many prestigious awards. We welcome you to explore the wealth of information available on Asia at **www.tuttlepublishing.com**.

Published by Tuttle Publishing, an imprint of Periplus Editions (HK) Ltd.

www.tuttlepublishing.com

ISBN: 978-4-8053-1921-5

Library of Congress Control Number: 2025938545

Distributed by

North America, Latin America & Europe
Tuttle Publishing
364 Innovation Drive
North Clarendon
VT 05759-9436, USA
Tel: 1 (802) 773 8930; Fax: 1 (802) 773 6993
info@tuttlepublishing.com
www.tuttlepublishing.com

Japan
Tuttle Publishing
Yaekari Building 3rd Floor
5-4-12 Osaki, Shinagawa-ku
Tokyo 141-0032
Tel: (81) 3 5437-0171; Fax: (81) 3 5437-0755
sales@tuttle.co.jp; www.tuttle.co.jp

Asia Pacific
Berkeley Books Pte. Ltd.
3 Kallang Sector #04-01
Singapore 349278
Tel: (65) 67412178; Fax: (65) 67412179
inquiries@periplus.com.sg
www.tuttlepublishing.com

GPSR representative
Matt Parsons
matt.parsons@upi2mbooks.hr
UPI-2M PLUS d.o.o.,
Medulićeva 20, 10000 Zagreb,
Croatia

28 27 26 25 5 4 3 2 1
Printed in China 2507CM